YOUCAT

YOUTH CATECHISM OF THE CATHOLIC CHURCH

STUDY GUIDE

JACK KERSTING • PAUL GEORGE

MARK BRUMLEY • VIVIAN W. DUDRO

IGNATIUS PRESS   **SAN FRANCISCO**

Nihil Obstat: Reverend Monsignor. J. Warren Holleran, S. T. D.
Imprimatur: ✝ Most Reverend Salvatore J. Cordileone, Archbishop of San Francisco
May 1, 2013

Cover and layout design: Riz Boncan Marsella
Interior Layout: Eloise Anagnost
Photography: Bill Wittman

CONTENTS

INTRODUCTION

Welcome to the YOUCAT *Study Guide*

Pope Benedict has asked you to study YOUCAT, which stands for *Youth Catechism of the Catholic Church*. YOUCAT is the first worldwide catechism specifically designed by and for young adults.

Though based on the *Catechism of the Catholic Church*, YOUCAT is written in a style and format just for you. It has been translated into multiple languages and distributed throughout the world. As a result, YOUCAT is having a profound effect on young Catholics everywhere, by helping them know and love Jesus Christ and the faith of the Church he founded.

And not a moment too soon, for, as Pope Benedict XVI writes in his foreword, Catholics need to know their faith now more than ever: "Yes, you need to be more deeply rooted in the faith than the generation of your parents so that you can engage the challenges and temptations of this time with strength and determination."

This *Study Guide* is designed to help you unpack YOUCAT from front to back. Its probing questions and thought-provoking exercises will help you read YOUCAT with understanding and joy, as you deepen your relationship with the God who loves you and has a plan for your happiness.

How to Use the *Study Guide*

The *Study Guide* is divided into the same four parts as YOUCAT, which are the same four pillars of the *Catechism of the Catholic Church*. Yes, there is a pattern here. Though the parts can be studied in any order, it is best to let the *Study Guide* lead you through YOUCAT by starting at the beginning and proceeding through each section as it comes.

The four main sections of both catechisms and of this *Study Guide* can be summed up as follows: what we believe, how we celebrate what we believe, how we live what we believe, and how we pray. For each of these sections, the *Study Guide* has several topics for study, discussion, further reflection, and application in your daily life.

With each topic, the first task is to read YOUCAT. To help you do this, there is a brief introduction to the topic (Behind YOUCAT), followed by a reading assignment (Read YOUCAT) and short-answer questions (What Does YOUCAT Say?). In the numbered paragraphs and along the margins of YOUCAT are quotations from the Bible. To help you read and reflect on these, there are a couple of questions about those passages, as well as some other important Bible texts (What Does the Bible Say?). Next, there are discussion questions that can be answered in either large or small groups (YOU Chat). For further reflection, there are some questions to answer either in your discussion group or on your own (YOU Reflect), followed by tasks for you to do in the coming week that will help you apply what you have learned (YOU Challenge).

PART 1

WHAT WE BELIEVE—EMBRACING AND LIVING THE TRUTH

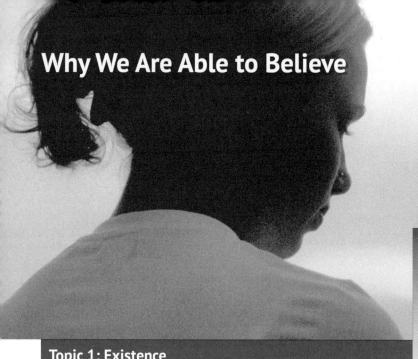

Why We Are Able to Believe

Topic 1: Existence

Behind YOUCAT

Why am I here? Where did I come from? What's my purpose in life? We all ask these questions about our existence. None of us is alone in wondering about the meaning of life. In fact, people have been asking these perplexing questions for thousands of years, and they have been looking for answers in religions and philosophies.

Read YOUCAT

Read nos. 1–2.

What Does YOUCAT Say?

1. What are the three things no. 1 says that God made us to do while we are on earth?
2. To help us find our way home to heaven, what did God do for us?
3. Based on no. 2, why did God make us and send Jesus to lead us to heaven?

What Does the Bible Say?

1. Who does Jesus say he is in John 14:6?
2. In his letter to Timothy (1 Tim 2:4), what does St. Paul say God desires?

YOU Reflect

God created us out of love—because he is love itself. True love desires the good of the one who is loved. God created us to be loved and to love by sharing in his goodness. He did this because he knew it would be good for us; he knew that this would make us happy. Ultimately, our lives only begin to make sense when we embrace the reality of God's love for us and his desire for us to love him in return—not for his sake but for ours.

1. What difference does it make for us and others when we firmly believe that God made us and loves us?
2. How does our hope in heaven affect the way we experience and live our lives on earth?
3. Have you ever loved someone who rejected your love? If so, how did it make you feel? If not, how do you suppose you would feel if it happened to you?

YOU Chat

1. Is there anything in no. 1 or no. 2 that is new to you? If so, what? If not, explain in your own words what these Q&As mean.

2. What is the most challenging thing for you to believe in no. 1 or no. 2? Why?

YOU Challenge

Remember: Remind yourself every day this week that God made you and loves you and wants you to know him and love him too.

Surrender: Each morning, give your day to God and ask him to guide you. Ask him to make his presence in your life real to you.

Notice: At the end of each day, take note of the good things God did for you and asked you to do through the circumstances of your life.

Man Is Receptive to God

awk-ward

Topic 2: Cravings, Desires, and Lattes

Behind YOUCAT

Do you ever get a craving for something? A pizza, a burger, or ice cream? Maybe a latte? Cravings or desires for food and drink are part of human life. We also have desires for other things—for example, for wealth, health, love, friendship, knowledge, and meaningful work. Most people would say they need such things to live well on earth—to be happy.

Of course people can also crave the wrong things—things harmful to them or too much of a good thing, which can wind up hurting them. What's more, even when people have what they need to be happy in this life, they find themselves unsatisfied on a deeper level. They want something more—a permanent, enduring happiness, and a relationship with someone who can make sense of everything and bring complete happiness.

Read YOUCAT

Read nos. 3, 281, and 285.

What Does YOUCAT Say?

1. What did St. Augustine say about our hearts?
2. Explain how fulfillment of desires in this life compares with that of the next life.
3. According to no. 285, what do we need in order to obtain the complete fulfillment of eternal happiness?

YOU Reflect

We all have longings. We were created with them. As a result of human sin, though, sometimes our longings mislead us. They can become disordered desires—desires for things that really harm us or desires for too much of something otherwise good for us. Desires may even conflict with each other, leaving us confused. Only through God can we completely sort out our longings and attain complete fulfillment. The Second Vatican Council said, "Man plunges into the depths of reality whenever he enters into his own heart; God, who probes the heart, awaits him there; there he discerns his proper destiny beneath the eyes of God" (*The Church in the Modern World*, no. 14). God awaits us in the depths of our hearts to help sort out our desires in order to fulfill our true purpose.

1. What is it that you are really looking for in the deepest desires of your heart?
2. How can you talk with God about your deepest longings?

What Does the Bible Say?

1. Read Galatians 5:16–24. When St. Paul refers to "the flesh" here, he doesn't mean simply "the human body"; he means the part of fallen human nature that allows the lower impulses of our bodily nature to dominate our good sense and to lead us into choosing bad things. What are the "works of the flesh" that St. Paul lists in Galatians 5:19–21?

2. What is the "fruit of the Spirit" he refers to in Galatians 5:22–23?

3. What does Psalm 37:4 say about the desires of our hearts?

YOU Chat

1. What is the most difficult thing about understanding cravings, desires, and longings?

2. Is there anything especially difficult for young people today when it comes to dealing with desires?

3. Is there comfort in knowing that there is an answer to satisfying your deepest longings? Explain.

YOU Challenge

Thank: Treat yourself to your favorite food or drink this week. Thank God for it and let it remind you of how God ultimately satisfies the human heart.

Ask: Write a letter to God about the deepest desires of your heart and ask him to fulfill those desires according to his wise plan for your life.

Seek: Give up a bad habit that only temporarily fulfills a desire. Seek God's help in overcoming the bad habit by replacing it with a good one.

God Approaches Us Men

Topic 3: The "Big Reveal"

Behind YOUCAT

You've probably watched a TV show in which there's a mysterious character whose identity the audience is longing to know. You may think you've got things figured out, but you're not certain. Finally, there's the all-important episode in which the truth is unveiled. Sometimes this unveiling is called "the big reveal". The story now makes more sense. You see the characters and their story in a whole new light, all because the mysterious character's identity has been revealed.

In some ways, God is like the mysterious character in a TV show. Throughout history people have had various ideas about him. Often sin has gotten in the way, and people have wound up making God out to be what they want him to be rather than coming to know him as he is. For this and other reasons, God chose to reveal certain things about himself. He did this gradually, until at last "the big reveal" came: Jesus Christ. Through Jesus, we come to know who God really is.

Read YOUCAT

Read nos. 5, 7, and 9–10.

What Does YOUCAT Say?

1. According to no. 5, what are reasons some people deny God exists?
2. Why did God reveal himself rather than leaving us to figure out on our own that he exists?

continued on next page

YOU Reflect

The word "reveal" is related to the word "revelation". God reveals himself to us—tells us about himself—in divine *revelation*. His fullest revelation is Jesus Christ, who is God and man, divine and human. When God reveals himself to us, he tells us about himself but also about ourselves—where we came from, what God desires for us, and what we can become. He told us as much about himself as we can receive when he came as one of us—Jesus.

1. Think about the word "God". What images come to mind? Then think about Jesus. Does thinking about Jesus change how you think about God? Why or why not?

2. What are ways that God has manifested himself in your life?

3. What difference does God's revelation in Jesus Christ make to your life—to the way you see the world, the choices you make, and what you hope for?

3. How did God accomplish his definitive revelation, according to no. 7? Why did he do it (no. 9)?

4. How are private revelations different from the revelation of Jesus Christ (no. 10)?

What Does the Bible Say?

1. Read John 1:1–18. According to John 1:18, how do we come to know God the Father?

2. What do you think Jesus meant when he said, "He who has seen me has seen the Father" (Jn 14:9)?

YOU Chat

1. How did God reveal himself to man?

2. What are ways God continues to make his presence known to us today?

3. How does the Church reveal God's presence to us?

4. How does God speak to us in Sacred Scripture?

YOU Challenge

Pray: Find time to go to Mass one additional day this week besides Sunday, as a way of saying Yes to God's revelation of himself in Jesus Christ.

Learn: Read John 17:1–26. Think about how Jesus' words there reflect his being the fullest revelation of God.

Decide: Think about what God's plan is for your life and decide that you want to do whatever God wants you to do.

Man Responds to God

Topic 4: Believing

Behind YOUCAT

Some people think having religious faith means believing things you know aren't true. But that's nonsense. If you believe in your friends—that you have faith in them—doesn't it mean you're confident in them, that you trust them? And isn't that trust a kind of *knowing* the truth about them, based on your experience and relationship with them? That's not believing something you know isn't true. If a friend tells you something about himself you couldn't have discovered on your own, and your friend is reliable and trustworthy, then you truly *know* something about him, even though you have to take his word for it. Christian faith is like that, too. It's a kind of *knowing* and a kind of *trusting* in God when it comes to his telling us about himself and about ourselves. Because this kind of believing is based on reasonable trust, it's not "blind faith", and it's certainly not believing something we know isn't true.

Read YOUCAT

Read nos. 20–22.

What Does YOUCAT Say?

1. According to no. 20, how should we respond to God?
2. What kind of heart does a person need in order to believe?
3. Explain the two meanings of "believe" given in the parachutist example of no. 21.

YOU Reflect

Faith is a *supernatural gift* of God. It's beyond our natural abilities. We can believe because God's Spirit enables us to do so. Faith also mysteriously involves our choice to respond to God and his revelation (his Word). When we believe, we say Yes to God. In this way, faith is a kind of giving ourselves back to God, in response to his gift of creating us and giving himself to us in revelation.

1. If faith is a divine gift, does this mean that those who don't believe have not been offered the gift? Why or why not?
2. In what way is believing in someone a kind of giving yourself to that person? How is believing what God has revealed a kind of giving oneself to him?

What Does the Bible Say?

1. According to Hebrews 11:1, what is faith?
2. What does St. Paul say in 2 Corinthians 5:7? What do you think he means?
3. How does John 3:16 link believing and Jesus?

YOU Chat

1. Which of the seven characteristics of faith in no. 21 do you find most difficult to understand?
2. Faith in our friends isn't absolute; we recognize they're not perfect and they can sometimes let us down. How is faith in God different from faith in our friends? Why?
3. Have you ever doubted your friends or have been tempted by circumstances to doubt them, only to discover you misunderstood the situation? How might this kind of experience apply to faith in God and the challenges of life?
4. Why do you think no. 21 describes faith as "knowledge" as well as "trust"?

YOU Challenge

Think and Pray: This week think about one part of the Catholic faith you find most difficult to accept. Ask God to help you understand and believe more deeply.

Learn: Ask a parent, priest, teacher, or other knowledgeable Catholic to help you understand the part of the Catholic faith you find most difficult to accept. Look up the YOUCAT references to the topic and read them. Be patient in discovering answers to your questions.

The Christian Profession of Faith

Topic 5: Standing for Something

Behind YOUCAT

"Those who stand for nothing", it has been said, "will fall for anything." Taking a stand for what we believe—for our creed—is important. Someone's "creed" is the summary of his basic beliefs. One way we Catholics stand for our faith is by making the Profession of Faith. We do this by reciting the Creed at Sunday Mass, and we literally "take a stand" as we stand to recite it. The Creed is something we profess as a group, but it should also be something each of us as individual persons stands by. This is why although *we together* believe the Creed at Mass we each say, "*I believe*".

Read YOUCAT

Read nos. 24–29.

What Does YOUCAT Say?

1. What are some reasons why the Church has summarized key beliefs in the form of creeds?
2. What are the two main creeds of the Church?
3. Identify the core Christian belief about which the creeds elaborate.

What Does the Bible Say?

1. What does Matthew 10:32–33 say about professing our faith in Jesus Christ?
2. Read 1 Corinthians 15:3–8 and 1 Timothy 3:16. How do these passages of Scripture resemble or include early creeds?

YOU Reflect

The Creed is more than a summary of Christian beliefs. When we recite it at Mass, the Creed is a prayer. We've just finished hearing the Word of God proclaimed in Scripture and explained in the homily. Now it's our turn to speak to God. The Profession of Faith is an opportunity to confess our faith before God and other people in the Church. It's also a chance to remind ourselves of who we are, what we believe, and why we're at Mass.

1. How might the act of reciting the Creed at Mass be different if all people in the congregation realized they were professing their faith before God himself?
2. Do you ever find your mind wandering while reciting the Creed at Mass? What might you do to overcome that problem?
3. How does the fact that reciting the Creed is both a prayer to God and a statement of our key beliefs show that faith in God is both a kind of trust and a form of knowing?
4. How can clarity about what one believes help a person avoid being misled?

YOU Chat

1. Besides the Catholic Church, do you belong to any groups that have statements of belief or ideals? Identify other organizations with creeds or creed-like statements.

2. What point does the Creed stress by starting with "I believe" rather than "We believe"?

3. How many times in the Creed do we say, "I believe"? Why do you think these words are used in the places they are, as opposed to being used with other beliefs mentioned in the Creed?

YOU Challenge

Remember: When you're at Mass this Sunday, make a point to remember that the Profession of Faith is a prayer addressed to God as well as a statement of personal commitment made with the congregation.

Read, Think, and Ask: Re-read no. 28 and no. 29 in YOUCAT. Think about the part of the Creed you understand the least or find most difficult to accept. Ask your pastor, a parent, a teacher, a youth leader, or another knowledgeable Catholic to explain it to you.

Memorize: If you haven't already done so, memorize the Creed.

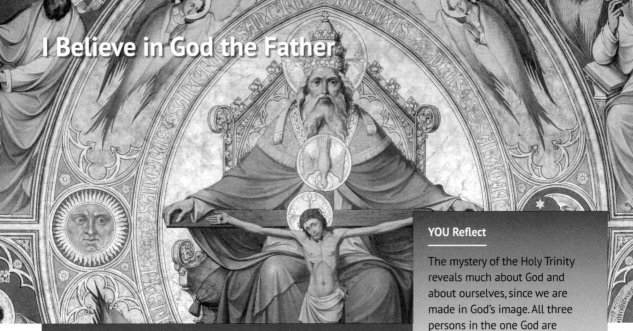

I Believe in God the Father

Topic 6: The Greatest Mystery

Behind YOUCAT

"It's a mystery!" When you hear those words, do you think of something we have blindly to accept? Or maybe you think of a problem to solve, as in a murder mystery? Divine mysteries are at the heart of Christianity. But divine mysteries aren't things we can say nothing about or puzzles to solve. They're profound realities that go beyond our limited powers to understand. Yet we can understand *something* about them, because God has told us about them, even though we can't understand *everything* about them. They're like an endless feast for the mind and the heart, as we go deeper and deeper into the truth. God himself is the greatest mystery. He is the one God, the Supreme Being—the One who is greater than anything else that can be thought of or imagined. And yet God has revealed himself as three divine persons: the Father, the Son, and the Holy Spirit—the Holy Trinity. God is one God, yet mysteriously there is a sense in which he is many (three divine persons). What's more, we're made in his image, so in order to understand ourselves, we must in some way understand him, mysterious though he is.

Read YOUCAT

Read nos. 30, 33, and 35–39.

YOU Reflect

The mystery of the Holy Trinity reveals much about God and about ourselves, since we are made in God's image. All three persons in the one God are *equal*—each is God. And yet each is *different and unique.* From all eternity, the Father "begets" the Son; the Son "comes from" the Father; and the Holy Spirit "proceeds" from both and unites both. Each is God, yet each is different. There is a hierarchy, or sacred order, in God's inner life that involves both *equality* and *difference.* This truth tells us that all human beings are in some way equal, yet they are also in various ways different and unique.

1. What does the mystery of the Holy Trinity tell us about the Son before the Incarnation?

2. In the Holy Trinity, all three persons are God and therefore are equal. Yet each person is unique—no one is interchangeable with or replaceable by the others. What does this mean for human persons—male and female—made in God's image?

3. To which of the three persons of the Holy Trinity do you seem closest? Why do you suppose this is so?

What Does YOUCAT Say?

1. According to no. 30, why can't there be more than one God, the supreme or highest being?
2. What is one consequence, according to no. 33, of the fact that God is love? How does he prove this?
3. Number 35 states that we know that God is triune (the Trinity) from Jesus Christ. How did Jesus reveal this?
4. How, according to no. 36, does the fact that God *is love* from all eternity tend to point to the truth that God is not alone and solitary but a Trinity of persons?
5. Why do we call God "Father"?
6. Who is the Holy Spirit?
7. How did the disciples come to recognize Jesus as the divine Lord and the second person of the Holy Trinity?

What Does the Bible Say?

1. In whose name is Baptism to be administered, according to Matthew 28:19?
2. How do John 1:1 and John 1:14 show that Jesus is God?
3. In light of God's revelation of the divine name in Exodus 3:14, how does Jesus' statement in John 8:58 point to his being God?
4. Read Acts 5:3, 32; Romans 8:27; and Ephesians 4:30. How do these passages indicate that the Holy Spirit is a divine person, not simply a force or energy?

YOU Chat

1. What features of our world seem most mysterious to you? Given the natural world's mysteries, is it surprising that the God who made the world would be mysterious?
2. What are some things implied by calling God "Father"?
3. What are some things implied by calling Jesus "the Son"?

YOU Challenge

Think: Reflect on each person of the Holy Trinity as you make the Sign of the Cross during prayers this week.

Ask: Pray that you may more deeply love the Triune God. Ask each person of the Trinity to help you better to know him.

Decide: Consider how you can act this week toward others based on the model of how the three persons of the Holy Trinity act toward one another. Resolve to act more "Trinitarian" this week.

I Believe in Jesus Christ, the Only Begotten Son of God

Topic 7: Disaster

Behind YOUCAT

Ever feel like everything is going perfectly well, and then, suddenly, disaster happens? And what about when the disaster is all your fault and it affects others besides you? That's how things started with the human race. God created the first man, Adam, in harmony with himself and the rest of creation. God formed the first woman, Eve, from Adam's side "bone" of his "bone" and "flesh" of his "flesh". Through the abuse of freedom, Adam's sin brought disorder to all man's relationships, with God, himself, his spouse, his family, and all creation. Adam's sin mysteriously affects all his descendants, all of us. What a disaster! Fortunately, though, God made the most of a bad situation. He was able to turn things around for our good.

Read YOUCAT

Read nos. 42, 51, 58, 63, and 67–70.

What Does YOUCAT Say?

1. Based on no. 42, explain the differences between how science approaches the question of human origins and how theology does. In what way may a Christian affirm the theory of evolution? What is evolutionism, and what is the Christian view of it?
2. According to no. 51, why does God allow evil to exist?
3. Explain the sense in which man is said to be created in God's image.
4. According to no. 63, what does it mean to say, "I have a soul"?
5. Explain the relationship among sin, the rejection of good, and the rejection of God.

continued next page

YOU Reflect

When we think of evil in the world, we're apt to focus on the issue of why bad things happen to good people. Seldom do we think about all the good we experience in the world and ask, "Why is there good?" And rarely do we consider all the good that exists in the world that would not have occurred, had not God allowed the abuse of freedom by his creatures. That is no excuse to do evil—as St. Paul said, we may not do evil in order for good to come about (Rom 6:1). But it does show the power of God to turn things around—to bring about good from evil.

1. Can you think of some good things God has brought about as a result of his permitting evil to exist? Would you exist today if no evil had ever been allowed to happen in human history? Explain.
2. If God is ultimate Good and good is the standard by which we discern whether something is evil, does it make sense to use the presence of evil in the world to argue against God's existence? It would seem that to call something "evil" only makes sense if there is something really "good". But if there is no God, in what sense can anything be really "good"? What do you think?

What Does YOUCAT Say? *continued*

6. Explain original sin, as described in no. 68. How does it differ for us from personal sin?

7. How did God overcome the problem of human sin?

What Does the Bible Say?

1. Read Genesis 1:31. What was the original condition of creation?

2. Read Genesis 1:26–28. To what does God link man's being made in his image?

3. Read Genesis 3:8. After our first parents disobeyed God, what did they do? Why do you suppose they did this?

4. Read Genesis 3:15. This passage contains a hidden prophecy of the Redeemer. How does it apply to Jesus and his Mother?

YOU Chat

1. Some Christians regard the theory of evolution as necessarily opposed to the doctrine of man's creation in God's image. The Catholic Church takes a different approach. What are the advantages of the Catholic approach? What are some challenges of that approach?

2. How does man's spiritual soul make him different from other animals? Does this justify our abuse of animals? Does our spiritual nature bring with it responsibility for creation? Explain.

3. What do you think is the biggest misunderstanding of the Christian belief in original sin?

YOU Challenge

Think and Ask: Think about someone who did something wrong but out of which others managed to bring about good. Ask God to help you be someone who brings good out of evil.

Confess: Go to confession this week.

I Believe in Jesus Christ, the Only Begotten Son of God

Topic 8: One of Us

Behind YOUCAT

If you're like most people, you probably like to think of your favorite celebrity as "one of us". Sure, there's a certain attraction to the glamor or fame or accomplishment of a celebrity, which most of us don't experience. But usually we want the celebrities we admire to share something with us, to be people we can on some level "relate to". Whether they really are, or only appear to be, "one of us" is another matter. It's not exactly right to think of God as a "celebrity". And the gap between God and us is infinite. Still, God loves us so much that he overcame the distance between him and us. The author of the story of history entered into history as one of the characters. In the Incarnation, God became "one of us" so that we could share in his life and his love. He, too, suffered and died, as we do. And he rose from the dead, so that one day we, too, may do so. In other words, he became "one of us" so that we could become like him—children of God.

Read YOUCAT

Read nos. 73, 76–77, 79–80, 101, 106, and 111.

What Does YOUCAT Say?

1. Many people think of "Christ" as Jesus' last name, but the word is really a title. What does it mean, according to no. 73, and how does it apply to Jesus?
2. According to no. 76, God became man. What does no. 77 also tell us about Jesus?
3. What does it mean to say that Jesus was born of the Virgin Mary? What is the significance of his conception in this way?

continued next page

YOU Reflect

Jesus is God. He is "consubstantial" with the Father, meaning they are both the one God. And yet our faith tells us that Jesus was truly "one of us"—a man. We say that Jesus is "true God and true man". Some people find it hard to believe that God came among us. Others find it difficult to think of Jesus as truly human, with the kind of human limitations other men have, only without sin. Thinking of Jesus as having a divine way of acting and a human way of acting can be difficult. But if we keep both truths about Christ together in our minds, the truth about his divinity and the truth about his humanity, then we can learn something about God and about ourselves. We see how much God loves us, despite the bad things we do to him and to one another. He loves us so much he became one of us. And we see that by turning away from sin and turning to God's love, we can become children of God through our relationship with Jesus. We can become like Jesus and therefore like God.

continued next page

What Does YOUCAT Say? *continued*

4. No. 101 discusses Jesus' crucifixion. Explain the significance of his death on a cross. Why crucifixion?
5. Explain the case for the Resurrection of Jesus as summarized in no. 106.

What Does the Bible Say?

1. Read John 1:1–18. What does this passage mean when it states, "And the Word became flesh and dwelt among us"?
2. How does Jesus' healing of the paralyzed man in Mark 2:1–12 point to his divine identity?
3. What does St. Paul say in Galatians 4:4–6 about God the Father's purpose in sending Jesus into the world?
4. What did Jesus teach about the end of the world in Matthew 24:36?
5. List those mentioned in 1 Corinthians 15:3–9 as among those who were eyewitnesses of the resurrected Jesus. What significance does Paul attach to Jesus' Resurrection in 1 Corinthians 15:14–19?

YOU Chat

1. Some people think of Jesus as only a good man or only a prophet but not the Son of God, whom he claimed to be. Yet if Jesus said and did the kind of things attributed to him in the Gospels, why do you think it would be false to say he was only a good man or only a prophet?
2. Jesus' closest disciples and friends saw him brutally executed at the hands of Israel's enemies. That is not what they expected to happen to the Messiah. How likely would it have been for Jesus' disciples to continue to proclaim him the Messiah and the Son of God if they had not seen him raised from the dead?
3. Some Christians put a great deal of emphasis on Jesus' second coming. Do you think it matters whether Jesus will return? Explain.

YOU Challenge

Pray: Ask Jesus to be a part of every aspect of your life.
Learn: Memorize John 1:1.
Visit: Make time this week to spend in prayer and reflection before the Blessed Sacrament.

YOU Reflect, *continued*

1. How do you think people's idea about God would have been different had Jesus not become one of us?
2. Would you say you have a "personal relationship" with Jesus?
3. How does the fact that Jesus is God affect how you think about his teaching?
4. When you are suffering, do you ever think about the fact that God himself also suffered, that he experienced the limitations of life in this world and even rejection by friends and suffered harm from his enemies?

I Believe in ... the Holy Spirit

Topic 9: Team Spirit

Behind YOUCAT

If you've ever been on a team, you know working together for a common goal can get people excited. There's a "team spirit", which sometimes takes over and which can bring people even closer together as they work to achieve their goal. In a way, the Church is like a team, Jesus' team. Our common goal is to help the world to know Jesus, to follow him, and to become God's children through Jesus. To equip us to achieve that goal, Jesus has given us his Spirit, the Holy Spirit. But the Holy Spirit is much greater than any "team spirit". He isn't the effect of our enthusiasm together. He is the One who unites us, energizes us, and equips us to achieve our goal.

Read YOUCAT

Read nos. 35, 113, 115, and 118–120.

What Does YOUCAT Say?

1. According to nos. 113 and 118–119, what role does the Holy Spirit play in the Church?
2. Identify some of the titles we give to the Holy Spirit (no. 115).
3. What place does the Holy Spirit have in the life of the individual believer (no. 120)?

YOU Reflect

Believers often think of themselves as praying to the Father. They may picture Jesus standing by their side and helping them to pray. But the Holy Spirit? Isn't he a dove? "How does a dove fit into my spiritual life?" someone might wonder. The Holy Spirit is God himself, not a dove. He manifested himself as a dove at Jesus' baptism in order to *symbolize* God's love. While all three divine persons of the Holy Trinity live within us by God's grace, we associate God's indwelling in a special way with the Holy Spirit. Why? Because he is the love between Father and Son in the Trinity. It makes sense that we would associate him with God's love within our hearts and God's love in bringing his people together in the Church.

1. Why do you think the Holy Spirit sometimes gets overlooked when we think about God?
2. Do you ever pray to the Holy Spirit? If so, what sort of things do you pray to him about? If not, why not?
3. Have you ever been in a situation in which you needed to rely on the Holy Spirit? Explain.

What Does the Bible Say?

1. What does Genesis 1:2 say about the Holy Spirit's role in creation? What does Genesis 2:7 say about man and God's breath (or Spirit)?
2. Explain Jesus' role with respect to the Holy Spirit (Lk 4:14–19; Acts 1:5).
3. What is the relationship between Baptism and the Holy Spirit (Jn 3:3–8; 1 Cor 12:13; Tit 3:5)?
4. How did the Holy Spirit show his presence among the apostles on the day of Pentecost (Acts 2:1–11)?
5. How does Paul see the Holy Spirit's part in prayer (Rom 8:26)?

YOU Chat

1. The Holy Spirit is involved with all seven sacraments of the Church, but with which sacrament do we especially associate his work?
2. Explain the effect the Holy Spirit had on the apostles on Pentecost. What did the Holy Spirit's presence among the apostles enable Peter to do (no. 118; Acts 2:14, 41)?
3. What are the fruits of the Holy Spirit (no. 311; Gal 5:22–23)?

YOU Challenge

Pray: Make a point of praying to the Holy Spirit himself each day this week. Ask the Holy Spirit to help you to be more aware of his presence.

Read: Look up the seven gifts of the Holy Spirit in no. 310. Think about which of those gifts seem most operative in your life.

Learn: Memorize the twelve fruits of the Holy Spirit (no. 311; Gal 5:22–23).

Ask: Pray to the Holy Spirit to endow you with his fruits to enable you to grow closer to God and to serve others.

I Believe in ... the Holy Catholic Church

Topic 10: Team Players

Behind YOUCAT

"Team Spirit" is another name for the Holy Spirit, but the "team" is the Church. As members of the Church, we're part of the team. That means we're supposed to be "team players"—we're supposed to work together for the good of the team. We're supposed to help one another to find God's specific purpose for our lives (our position on the team). Of course, like a team, the Church has different roles for people. But, also like a team, there is a role every player has—to help the team win. The way we "win" in the Church is, ultimately, by getting to be with God forever and by helping as many other people as we can to do so too. Meanwhile, we begin to taste the team "victory" in this life. We grow in holiness—love for God and love for others. We try to influence our world for God. Jesus is the head of the team. The team's heroes are the saints, the winners of past victories. And the team's officers are the clergy, religious leaders, and lay leaders. Each of us has a position to play, so that the team can play its best.

Read YOUCAT

Read YOUCAT nos. 121–124, 126–127, 129, 138, and 141.

What Does YOUCAT Say?

1. According to no. 121, what are some different ways to describe the Church?
2. Why did God establish the Church, and what is the Church's mission (nos. 122–123)?

continued next page

YOU Reflect

When you think of the Church, do you picture a building? Or maybe the Pope, the bishops, priests, deacons, and religious sisters and brothers? Or do you think of the whole People of God, laity as well as clergy and religious? Although we're part of the Church, we sometimes forget what the Church really is. Sometimes a group of people will say, "We are the Church." In fact, no *one* group in the Church is *the Church*. The Church is the *whole* People of God—those on earth now, the souls in purgatory being purified for heaven, and those with God now in heaven. And the Church is made up of her ordained leaders, members of religious communities, and the laity. *Together* we are the Church.

1. When do you most *feel* that you are part of the Church? Why?
2. Whether or not you *feel* a part of the Church, to what can you point to have confidence you *are*?
3. Do you think the Pope or your pastor belongs to the Church *more* than you do? Explain your answer.
4. St. Joan of Arc said to her inquisitors: "The Church is Christ." How is this true? In what way is it not true?

What Does YOUCAT Say? *continued*

3. Explain how the Church is like a body (no. 126) and like a bride (no. 127).

4. According to no. 129, how many churches are there?

5. What is the difference between the laity and the clergy in the Church (no. 138)?

What Does the Bible Say?

1. Read 1 Corinthians 12:12–26. To what does St. Paul compare individual Christians in the Church? In what sense is it the case that if one member of the Church suffers, all members suffer?

2. How does St. Paul describe Christ and the Church in Ephesians 2:19–22 and 5:25–32?

3. What does Matthew 16:18–19 tell us about the Church Jesus established?

4. What is the mission of the Church, according to Matthew 28:19–20 and Acts 1:8?

5. What does Jesus say about his disciples in John 13:35? How does this help his followers fulfill the mission of the Church?

YOU Chat

1. Why do you suppose there are so many different images to describe the Church?

2. How is the Church like a team?

3. Given what Jesus and St. Paul said about the Church, should we be surprised that there have been great saints and great sinners in the Church? Why or why not?

4. If Jesus founded only one Church, why are there so many different groups of Christians, with different beliefs, ways of worship, and kinds of leadership?

5. What is the main way lay people live as disciples of Jesus?

YOU Challenge

Pray: Pray for the various leaders in the Church—the Pope, your bishop, your parish priests and deacons, religious (sisters or brothers in religious orders), and lay leaders.

Learn: Discover the name of the bishop of your diocese (if you don't already know it).

Think and Ask: Think about God's putting you on the "team" of the Church. Reflect on your gifts and talents. Ask God to show you what "position" he has for you on the "team".

I Believe in ... the Holy Catholic Church

Topic 11: What Else Is There?

Behind YOUCAT

When the American novelist Walker Percy was asked why he became a Catholic, his reply was, "What else is there?" You and I might be tempted to reply, "Plenty." But, ultimately, is that so? If God is *real* and we were made for happiness with him, in the end there really isn't anything else. Everything else must be understood in light of God, who alone can make us truly happy. Blessed Charles de Foucauld said, "After I recognized there is a God, it was impossible for me not to live for him alone." In the end, the persons and things of this life either take us back to God, or they take us away from him. Those who recognize this and commit themselves accordingly we call saints.

Read YOUCAT

Read nos. 84–85, and 147–150.

What Does YOUCAT Say?

1. According to no. 146, what is the communion of saints?
2. Number 147 describes the Assumption; what happened to Mary at the end of her life?
3. Can Mary really help us more than any other saint (nos. 147–148)?
4. How can a priest forgive sins (no. 150)?

YOU Reflect

How well do you know the saints? Can you picture yourself becoming a saint? For some people, even for some Catholics, the idea of becoming a saint seems boring. Yet the *Lives of the Saints* are filled with very different and universally fascinating people. All of us are made for happiness, and in studying their lives we find—though they often struggled to overcome personal weakness and sin—the saints are the only truly happy persons. More to the point, each of us will ultimately return to God and therefore become saints, or we will face eternity without God—and thus, without meaning, purpose, love, or happiness. So let's get started now on becoming saints ourselves!

1. When you think of the idea of a saint, what images come into your mind? Why?
2. What do you think is the biggest mistake people make about saints?
3. How are ultimate happiness and being a saint linked together?

What Does the Bible Say?

1. Read Ephesians 4:14–16. How must we live to be built up in love?
2. Read John 2:1–12. How does the wedding at Cana reveal Mary's role in the lives of Jesus' followers? What does Mary tell us servants to do?
3. Read Luke 1:46–55. What do we call this prayer? How have Mary's words been fulfilled and continue to be fulfilled in the Church today?

YOU Chat

1. Is everyone called to be a saint?
2. With whom are we in "communion"? How do we live out and intensify that communion?
3. Who is Mary in your life?
4. What is the Rosary, and how can it help us become holy (no. 149)?

YOU Challenge

Pray: Pray the Rosary with your family this week or on your own for the souls in purgatory.

Learn: Memorize the mysteries of the Rosary.

Ask: Pray to your guardian angel and your patron saint, asking them to help you know and love them and Jesus better.

Go: Confess your sins to a priest this week, especially if it has been longer than a month since you last received the sacrament of Reconciliation. Start doing good!

I Believe in ... the Holy Catholic Church

Topic 12: And Then There Were Four ...

Behind YOUCAT

Death, judgment, heaven, and hell: the Four Last Things. We are all going to die; there's no way out alive! At the moment of death we will be judged. That sounds ominous! The Good News is the One doing the judging has done everything possible to see you make it safely to heaven, and eternal joy. He "desires all men to be saved ..." (1 Tim 2:4). He took on "flesh" not only to suffer death in the "flesh" for us, but to redeem us, body and soul. When we die in God's friendship, we enter eternal life. If we are ready and able to love as he loves, we fall right into his arms. If we love imperfectly, we will need purification (purgatory) to be made into a perfect lover. All the persons in heaven— the Triune God, the saints, and the angels—love perfectly and are perfectly loved. That's why heaven is such an awesome place of joy beyond anything we can imagine, with no hurts, no sorrow, no shame, no loneliness—pure, joyful, love in union with everyone we could ever want to be with, forever. Amen.

Read YOUCAT

Read nos. 1, 3, and 152–164.

What Does YOUCAT Say?

1. What happens at death? What will happen to our bodies at the end of time (nos. 153–154 and 163)?
2. What is eternal life? How do we know it is what we were made for (nos. 1, 3, and 156)?
3. What is purgatory (no. 159)?
4. Is there a hell? If so, who goes there (nos. 161–162)?

YOU Reflect

If this world and our part in it simply end in death, life really makes no sense at all. However, God did not leave us in the dark about life and death. He sent his only begotten Son to show us the way through death to eternal life. Jesus said he was God the Son, and he said he would suffer, die, and rise from the dead. The fact of his Resurrection shows he is who he says he is: God-made-man. The reality of the Resurrection is reason enough for us to take Jesus at his word. He is our Way, our Truth, and our Life. When are we going to start living for him, our risen Lord? When do we start the revolution? As St. Philip Neri used to ask his young friends in Rome who helped him reevangelize the city of Peter and Paul at a time of scandalous corruption, "When are we going to start doing good?"

1. What matters more, how one begins or how one finishes in life?
2. When it comes to "doing good", can we do the right thing for the wrong reason? How do you think such things will appear on the Day of Judgment?

What Does the Bible Say?

1. Read 1 Corinthians 15:13–20. Why are we to be pitied if Christ did not rise from the dead?
2. Read 1 Corinthians 15:35–37. Do we know how the resurrection takes place? What *do* we know about it?
3. Read 1 Corinthians 13:12. What is meant by the beatific vision?
4. According to Matthew 25:31–46, on what basis will we be judged?

YOU Chat

1. How do we know Jesus' Resurrection happened? What is the evidence for it?
2. Why will the beatific vision make us happy beyond what we can possibly imagine?
3. St. John of the Cross says that "we shall be judged on love." How can that be reconciled with Matthew 25?

YOU Challenge

Pray: Meditate on and repeat ten to twenty times one day this week the third memorial acclamation of the Mass: "Save us, Savior of the world, for by your Cross and Resurrection, you have set us free."

Read: Go online to www. MagisReasonFaith.org and read the amazing scientific studies of people who have had "near death" experiences (click on Other Resources tab).

Memorize: Look up Romans 14:8 (p. 95 of YOUCAT) and C. S. Lewis' quote on top of p. 96 of YOUCAT. Write these words on your heart and live by them.

PART 2

HOW WE CELEBRATE THE CHRISTIAN MYSTERIES— DISCOVERING THE SACRED

God Acts in our Regard by Means of Sacred Signs

Topic 1: STOP!

Behind YOUCAT

Have you ever had the experience of driving around, minding your own business, and before you even had a chance to put on the brakes, a STOP sign reached out and grabbed your car and made it stop? Probably not, huh?

Well, that would have been quite unusual for a stop sign. A stop sign, like every other sign, communicates a message, but like most signs, it cannot bring about what it signifies. That's just how sacred signs, the sacraments, differ from other signs. They actually do what they signify; in other words, sacramental signs are efficacious. They bring into effect what they represent.

When the water was poured over your head at Baptism, you were cleansed of all sin. When the words "I baptize you in the name of the Father, and of the Son, and of the Holy Spirit" were said at the same time as the water was poured, you became a member of God's family, and the very life of God was poured into you; you were born again as a child of God. A sacrament, Baptism, did this. Sacraments are the most powerful signs in the world!

Read YOUCAT

Read nos. 166–169.

Read nos. 166–169.

YOU Reflect

Often we do things without thinking. We may do something out of habit. When the habit is a good one, we call it a virtue. When it's a bad habit, we call it a vice. Taking part in Mass without thinking about it or without paying attention is a bad habit we can fall into. To overcome a bad habit, spiritual writers say we ought to replace it with a good one. A good habit to develop in order to participate better in Mass is to concentrate on the readings and the prayers.

1. Have you ever felt "bored" during the sacred liturgy? Why do you think that happens sometimes? What can be done about it?
2. What are some simple things you might do to prevent distractions at Mass?
3. Do you ever dress or behave in a way that distracts others at Mass?

What Does YOUCAT Say?

1. What does Pope Benedict say about the immensity of the liturgy (p. 102, margin)?
2. What is liturgy, and why should we want to participate (p. 102, margin, and nos. 166 and 167)?
3. Why do the liturgy and sacraments play such an important role in the life of the Church and the life of each of us as members of the Church (nos. 168 and 169)?

What Does the Bible Say?

1. What did Jesus say about himself in John 14:6? How are the sacraments efficacious signs of the life and power of Jesus?
2. Read Luke 6:19. How does what happens in this passage relate to the liturgy and the sacraments?
3. According to John 10:7–11 and 14–18, for whose benefit, at whose command, and for what purpose did Jesus come? What does the liturgy have to do with it?

YOU Chat

1. What does the Sunday Eucharist have to do with my life and the life of the world?
2. Why do you think St. Benedict said, "Nothing may have priority over the liturgy"?
3. Why does he consider the liturgy so important?

YOU Challenge

Resolve: Eliminate any boredom you might feel on Sunday by forgetting yourself at Mass and focusing on Jesus and his invitation to live life more fully.

Prepare: Resolve to remember and think about the Gospel that is read at Sunday Mass.

Pray: Ask for eyes to see the truth of the Good News Jesus has revealed and shared with us in the liturgy.

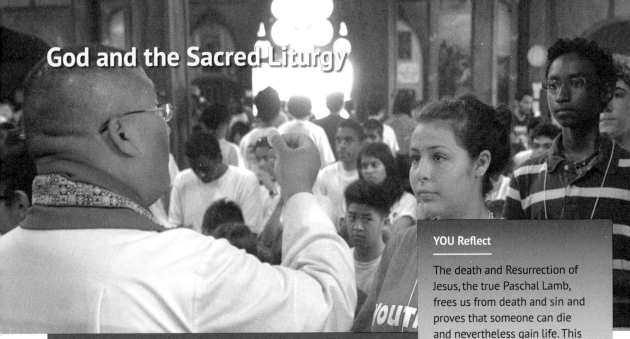

God and the Sacred Liturgy

Topic 2: The Family Feast

Behind YOUCAT

Does your extended family gather together for Thanksgiving? Do you get out the best silver, the best china, set the table with an elegant tablecloth? For most, the preparations for the feast are an all-day affair. The food is the best ever, especially the desserts! It is a time of great anticipation and satisfaction.

In God's family, there is a feast as well. And every Sunday is a day of Thanksgiving. God is the host, and the feast is the sacred liturgy. God personally invites us to become part of his Family. He guides his Church to take great care and effort to put on the best feast, with costly vestments and holy vessels, and the finest food available to man: God himself.

The Bible says man lives on "every word that proceeds from the mouth of God" (Mt 4:4). In the liturgy, God speaks his Word and gives life to his family. In the Mass, God shows the depth of his love for us by mysteriously making present the saving sacrifice of his Son, who then feeds us with his very self.

Read YOUCAT

Read nos. 170–171, 173, and 175–178.

The death and Resurrection of Jesus, the true Paschal Lamb, frees us from death and sin and proves that someone can die and nevertheless gain life. This life, his risen life, he shares with us through the liturgy and the sacred signs of the sacraments. Frequent and worthy reception of Christ's sacraments causes us to outgrow our human pettiness and become fully human and fully alive as Jesus, the God-man, is.

The sacraments are not magic. Faith is one prerequisite for our receiving the full benefits of the sacraments. Do we receive with faith? Do we receive in the state of grace those sacraments that require it? Will we strive all the more in the future to believe in the One who empowers every sacrament, and will we receive them humbly and gratefully, abandoning ourselves to the will and presence of God? Our holiness, happiness, and eternity are at stake. Will we choose to love and receive love from the One who gave everything for us?

1. How is faith important in order to receive God's grace in the sacraments?

continued on next page

What Does YOUCAT Say?

1. Why must our earthly liturgies be celebrations full of beauty and power (nos. 170–171)?
2. What is the most important liturgy in the world (no. 171)?
3. How does each sacrament fulfill a particular human need (no. 173)?
4. Why is faith a needed part of receiving the sacraments (no. 177)?

What Does the Bible Say?

1. In so many of the Psalms of the Bible used in the Catholic liturgy, like Psalm 43:5, we are encouraged to praise the Lord. Why do people need to praise the Lord?
2. In the Book of Exodus, we read of the Passover of the Jewish people from Egypt. Exodus 12 tells us of the paschal lamb and his blood. What do they prefigure?

YOU Chat

1. How does God bless us in the liturgy, and how does it remind us that the fact we exist is something beautiful?
2. What does it mean to say a sacramental sign does what it signifies?
3. Which of the seven sacraments is the most important? Which one would you say is next in importance? Give your reasons.

YOU Challenge

Study: Each sacrament has its unique purpose. Study what YOUCAT says about the purpose of the sacrament of Reconciliation.

Receive: Commit yourself to frequent reception of the sacrament of Reconciliation—once a week, once every two weeks, or at least once a month. Be reconciled to God!

Prepare: Make sure you are in the state of grace, prayerfully read the Sunday Gospel, and beg Jesus to help you love him before receiving Holy Communion this Sunday.

Thank: Take ten minutes to thank Jesus with all your heart once you have received him in Holy Communion at Mass this Sunday.

YOU Reflect, *continued*

2. Which sacraments do not require our being in the state of grace to receive them?
3. In what ways is someone more apt to treat the sacraments as if they were magic if he does not have a close relationship with Christ?

How We Celebrate the Mysteries of Christ

Topic 3: Date Time

Behind YOUCAT

Have you ever planned a date with a special friend, someone you haven't seen enough, but you'd really like to know better? One thing you must do: set a time and a place where both of you can get together to enjoy each other's company. God wants to be your best friend, and he is well worth getting to know. No one can love you like he can! But you need a time and place to meet that you can count on. Sunday is the day, and your parish church is the place. This is our special time to meet with God. He is there waiting. God is not just some impersonal force found anywhere and everywhere. He is personal, and he wants to be your personal friend. He wants you to be able to share your hopes, dreams, fears, and problems. You can do that anywhere, of course, but there is something special about meeting with him at Sunday Mass.

Read YOUCAT

Read nos. 179, 182, 184–187, and 189–190.

What Does YOUCAT Say?

1. In what way is Christ the main one who celebrates the liturgy (no. 179)?
2. Into what do we enter in celebrating the liturgy (Pope Benedict, p. 108, margin)?
3. How does God affect earthly time in the liturgy (nos. 184–188)?
4. If we can worship God anywhere, why is it important to have sacred places such as churches (nos. 189–190)?

YOU Reflect

God is everywhere. If so, why do we build churches as special places to be with God? One reason is for us to have a place to come together as a community to be with God and acknowledge him. Another is to remind ourselves that God is greater than the world in which we find him. He is its source. To symbolize that, we "consecrate" certain places and times as specially representative of God. These are "sacred" or "set apart" from our everyday places and times, which means we treat them as different. They are reminders that our ordinary places and times all flow from God. Sunday Mass at church is an example. The Sunday liturgy should be the place and time from which, in a sense, all of the coming week's activities begin—with God as the source of all we do. It should also be the place and time back to which all the previous week's activities should be brought, in offering to the Lord.

continued next page

What Does the Bible Say?

1. How does the Catholic liturgy fill the earth with God's glory as proclaimed in Isaiah 6:3?
2. St. Augustine says he who sings well prays twice. Read Ephesians 5:18–20. What does St. Paul urge us to do in this Bible passage?
3. Jesus founded one Church and gave her the liturgy, as affirmed in Ephesians 4:5–6. How can we best participate in the Church and her liturgy?

YOU Chat

1. Discuss the differences in the way a priest participates in Christ's divine worship and a lay person participates.
2. Why does man need signs, symbols, and words to understand reality?
3. What is sacred music? What kind of music moves our hearts deeply and brings us closer to God?

YOU Challenge

Memorize: Learn the five liturgical seasons and their significance.

Visit: Once this week go to see Jesus present in the tabernacle in church and ask him to help you enter more fully into his liturgy and sacraments.

Prepare: Before the next Sunday Mass, read the Gospel for that day and ask Jesus what he wants you to learn.

YOU Reflect, *continued*

1. When you attend Mass on Sundays, do you bring the activities of the previous week to the Lord, as part of your "offering" to him? Do you offer him the activities of the coming week?
2. To "consecrate" means to "set apart for God". In what way is space "consecrated" in a church? How is time "consecrated" for Catholics?

Sacraments of Initiation—Baptism and Confirmation

Topic 4: New in Town?

Behind YOUCAT

Most of us have had the experience of joining something or being the "newbie". Maybe we've moved into a new town, neighborhood, or school. Maybe we're the new guy on the team or in the club. In all these situations, we've gone through a process, initiating us into something new. We come to belong to a new community; we come to share its values, commitments, even ways of acting and thinking. Jesus set up a way we could come to belong to his Church. He instituted three sacraments of initiation—Baptism, Confirmation, and Holy Eucharist—which make us belong truly and more and more to him and his Church. The first two of these sacraments, Baptism and Confirmation, complement one another. By Baptism, we are made members of the Church. By Confirmation, we grow ever more deeply in Christ and become an evermore productive member of his Church.

Read YOUCAT

Read nos. 193–194, 199–200, 203, and 205–206.

What Does YOUCAT Say?

1. According to Pope Benedict XVI, what happens when a child is baptized (p. 116)?
2. Identify the seven sacraments (no. 193).
3. What are the three sacraments of initiation, and what unites them to one another (no. 193)?
4. How is Baptism the "gateway" sacrament (nos. 194 and 199–200)?
5. What is Confirmation, and what happens in Confirmation (nos. 203 and 205–206)?

YOU Reflect

You may have been baptized as an infant. If so, you don't remember it. It was something done *for you*, as so many other things have been done *for* you. As you grow older, what was done *for* you must become something *you take responsibility for*. As your parents gave you life and you must now decide how to live it, so, too, as an infant you may have been given spiritual life in Baptism and you must now decide for yourself to follow Christ. Perhaps you have recently received Confirmation, in which case those gifts have been strengthened. Or if you haven't yet been confirmed, perhaps you will soon. The point is, now you must answer for yourself. You must take responsibility for your spiritual life and destiny.

1. Would you be more comfortable telling a stranger that you were baptized or telling him that you are a Christian, a follower of Jesus Christ? Is there a difference? Why or why not?

continued next page

What Does the Bible Say?

1. Explain how 2 Corinthians 5:17 is really talking about the sacrament of Baptism.
2. Read Matthew 28:18–20. When did Jesus say this and to whom? Does it mean Baptism is very important, somewhat important, or of little importance?
3. According to John 3:5, how important and necessary is Baptism?
4. To which sacrament does Acts 8:14–16 refer?

YOU Chat

1. Why, do you think, is faith required for Baptism? Are there exceptions? Explain.
2. Why don't individuals have to wait until they are old enough to choose Baptism for themselves?
3. Should every baptized Catholic be confirmed? Explain.

YOU Challenge

Thank: Take a moment this week to tell God "thank you" for the gift of Baptism and for his making you his child through Baptism.

Seek: Find a Catholic at your school or in your neighborhood who has yet to be confirmed. Invite him and encourage him to go and see if he wants to follow Christ.

Pray: Recite the prayer "Come, Holy Spirit": *Come, Holy Spirit, fill the hearts of your faithful and enkindle in them the fire of your love. Send forth your Spirit, and we shall be created, and you shall renew the face of the earth. O, God, who by the light of the Holy Spirit, did instruct the hearts of the faithful, grant that by the same Holy Spirit we may be truly wise and ever enjoy his consolation. Through Christ our Lord. Amen.*

Visit: Sometime this week, visit a person who is sick or elderly and spend some time listening, talking, and being present.

YOU Reflect, *continued*

2. Some non-Catholic Christians don't believe in infant Baptism because they want each believer to make an adult commitment to follow Christ. What gifts does this outlook deprive children of? How can the concern for an adult commitment be addressed without giving up infant Baptism?
3. Baptism is the beginning of Christian life. But just because it has begun doesn't mean it will continue. Are you committed to continuing to follow Jesus Christ?

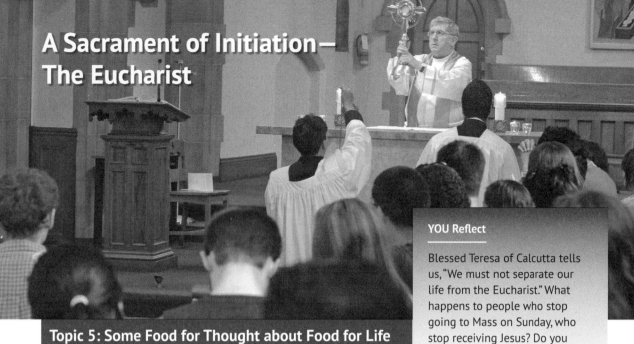

A Sacrament of Initiation—The Eucharist

Topic 5: Some Food for Thought about Food for Life

Behind YOUCAT

You know that if you don't eat, you don't live—at least not for long. The body needs nutrition. Our body assimilates the nutrients in food and uses them to build and power our cells. It's not far-fetched to say, "You are what you eat." The food Jesus gives us in the Eucharist is real food. It is nourishment, but not for our bodies—it's for our souls. And instead of us assimilating Jesus into ourselves and somehow making him like us, just the opposite happens. We become like him. Our souls "take in" this Living Food, but it is our souls that are really "taken up into" him. We become other Christs—sort of "little Christs". In other words, *Christians*. And then we are sent by him to be bread, food, for a spiritually starving world.

Read YOUCAT

Read nos. 208, 210–211, 216–217, and 220–221.

What Does YOUCAT Say?

1. What is the Holy Eucharist (no. 208)?
2. What does the word "Eucharist" mean, and why is it called this (see p. 123, margin)?
3. Why is the Eucharist so important for the Church (no. 211)?
4. In what way does Christ himself lead the celebration of the Eucharist (no. 215)?
5. In what way is Christ present when the Eucharist is celebrated (no. 216)?
6. How does the Church become the Body of Christ (no. 217)?

YOU Reflect

Blessed Teresa of Calcutta tells us, "We must not separate our life from the Eucharist." What happens to people who stop going to Mass on Sunday, who stop receiving Jesus? Do you think they can really be happy without him? Jesus says, "Apart from me you can do nothing" (Jn 15:5).

1. What message is Christ sending us by his coming to us under the forms or appearances of bread and wine?
2. How can we describe "receiving" Jesus in the Eucharist as a kind of "giving"? What is "given", by whom and to whom?

What Does the Bible Say?

1. According to 1 Corinthians 11:23–29, when did Jesus institute the Eucharist? Of what are we guilty if we receive Holy Communion in an unworthy manner?
2. Hebrews 10:19–25 refers to Jesus as our High Priest. What does it tell us about the Eucharistic liturgy on earth?
3. Read Romans 8:31–39. How do we know we cannot possibly lose if we seek God and trust in him?

YOU Chat

1. Comment on this quote from St. Augustine (p. 124, margin): "I heard a voice from on high: I am the food of the strong; eat then of me and grow. But you will not transform me into yourself like food for the body, but rather you will be transformed into me."
2. What did St. Thomas Aquinas mean when he said, "The actual effect of the Eucharist is the transformation of man into God" (p. 123, margin)?

YOU Challenge

Practice: Begin this week, at least once a day, to ask our Eucharistic Lord to come into your soul to feed your hunger, and then thank him for all he has done for you. This is sometimes called a "spiritual communion".

Meditate: Each day for a week prayerfully consider the words of St. Thomas, "My Lord and my God", while picturing the risen Jesus standing before you, offering himself to you.

Go: Attend a weekday Mass as well as Sunday Mass, if your schedule allows, asking Jesus to increase your desire for him in the Holy Eucharist.

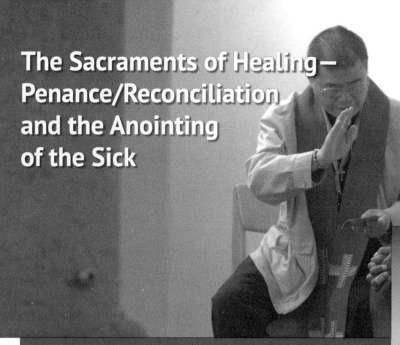

The Sacraments of Healing—Penance/Reconciliation and the Anointing of the Sick

Topic 6: Heal the Sin-Sick Soul

Behind YOUCAT

You know how it feels to be sick. Perhaps you have been so sick you could hardly move. Sickness limits our power to live. Depending on what kind of sickness is involved, it can also spread to others and harm them. Sin is a kind of sickness. As the body doesn't function well when it's sick, so the soul doesn't operate correctly when we have sinned. But unlike physical sickness, which may or may not be something we're responsible for, sin is a "sickness" we bring on ourselves. Although sickness doesn't necessarily mean the sick person himself has sinned, sickness in our world is one of the consequences of original sin, the sin of our first parents. Jesus had compassion for those wounded by sin, illness, and incapacity. In his day, he healed people and forgave sins. Today, he still sometimes heals people, and he always forgives those who are sorry for their sins. He gave us the sacraments of healing— Anointing of the Sick and Reconciliation (or Penance).

Read YOUCAT

Read nos. 224, 226–228, 233, 238–239, 241–243, and 245–246.

What Does YOUCAT Say?

1. Why did Christ institute two sacraments of healing (nos. 224, 226, and 243)?
2. If God alone forgives sins, how can a priest do so in the sacrament of Reconciliation (no. 228)?
3. What is the seal of the confessional (no. 238)?
4. Explain the positive effects of confession (no. 239).

YOU Reflect

When Jesus began his public mission, he said: "Repent, and believe in the gospel" (Mk 1:15). The call to follow Christ is a call to turn away from ourselves and our sins, and toward the one who brings the Gospel—the Good News of salvation and forgiveness. You can leave the old self behind and turn to Jesus by the power of the sacrament of Penance, which gives us the grace to examine ourselves, confess our sins, and experience forgiveness and reconciliation with God our Father. We are strengthened to stay true to our good intentions and leave ways of sin behind. Our God is merciful; he knows our need, and he wants to heal us in all the ways we need healing. We need to cast our cares upon the Lord and use those powerful sacraments he gave for our everlasting benefit.

1. How are the sacraments of Anointing of the Sick and Penance similar? How are they different?
2. Taking care of your body can help prevent physical sickness. What sort of things can we do to prevent the spiritual sickness of sin?

5. Explain why the Church cares for sick people (nos. 241–242).
6. Who may receive the Anointing of the Sick, and how does it work (nos. 243–246)?

What Does the Bible Say?

1. According to Luke 19:10 and Mark 2:17, why did Jesus come into the world?
2. Read 1 John 1:8. How does the sacrament of Penance fight against our tendency to self-deception?
3. In Luke 15:11–32, we read the story of the Prodigal Son. How does the story teach us about preparation for, and the effects of, a good confession?
4. Which sacrament did Jesus institute in John 20:22–23, and when did he do it?
5. In James 5:14, to what sacrament does St. James refer, and who are the "elders" of the Church?

YOU Chat

1. Do you experience any burdens in your life? Do you long to be completely unburdened, renewed in strength, and have a clean, new page in the book of your life? Do you think frequent confession is worth a try?
2. How does one make a good examination of conscience?
3. Does Jesus really want to heal you? Why does he not just heal everybody in one swoop? For whom did he institute the sacrament of the Anointing of the Sick?

YOU Challenge

Confess: At least once a month, take advantage of the sacrament of Penance to renew your soul and your strength, to lay claim to the mercy of Jesus.

Examine: Begin today to commit five minutes each day to an examination of conscience. There are probably some helpful booklets in the back of your parish church to walk you through this time of reflection. Or else you can ask your pastor or youth minister for help.

Pray: Each day this week, pray for those who are sick and those who are dying.

The Sacraments of Communion and Mission—Holy Orders and Marriage

Topic 7: No More Me, Myself, and I

Behind YOUCAT

Have you had the experience of doing something for someone else with nothing in it for you? Whenever we do something like that, we get very close to loving the way God loves, and knowing the joy he knows. It's not easy to act selflessly. The Fall has made us tend to have an attitude of *me, myself, and I*, aka *me first*. Jesus gave the Church two special sacraments that help us get out of ourselves and live for others: Matrimony and Holy Orders. These are called sacraments of communion and mission. They are both directed to the good of others. A man is ordained not just for himself, and no one enters the married state merely for his own sake. These two sacraments build up the People of God; they are channels through which God pours out love into the world and helps each one of us start to experience the joy of forgetting ourselves and loving as Christ loves.

Read YOUCAT

Read nos. 249–251 and 257–259.

What Does YOUCAT Say?

1. What does it mean to be an ordained Catholic priest (nos. 249–250)?
2. What are the degrees of the sacrament of Holy Orders (nos. 251–255)?
3. Why can only baptized and confirmed men receive Holy Orders (nos. 256–257)?
4. Why celibacy? What's wrong with priests getting married (no. 258)?

continued next page

YOU Reflect

It may seem as if the sacraments of Holy Orders and Matrimony are almost opposite to each other. Bishops and priests must be male and are generally unmarried. Married people are of opposite genders—men and women. But in a way, these sacraments are very similar. Both sacraments concern others and serve to bring others to know God—which is why they are sacraments of communion. Celibate bishops and priests are married—to the Church, as Christ himself is Bridegroom of the Church, which is his Bride. Bishops and priests share in Christ's husbandly role in relation to the Church. The sacrament of Matrimony helps spouses experience the sort of marital oneness Christ has with his Church.

1. Have you ever thought of priests as being "married" to the Church? How does this idea affect the discussion of such things as the male-only priesthood and priestly celibacy?
2. Individual believers can be male or female. But what "gender" do we usually think of the Church as a whole as being? What gender-specific terms do we often use for the Church? Why?

What Does YOUCAT Say? *continued*

5. Through Baptism, Christ has made each of us priestly; how is that different from the ordained priesthood (no. 259)?

6. St. Thomas teaches: "Priestly ordination is administered as a means of salvation . . . for the whole Church" (p. 143, margin). How does the whole Church benefit from one solitary priest?

What Does the Bible Say?

1. According to 1 Timothy 2:4–5, how does Christ continue to be our priest and one Mediator today?

2. What words of Jesus to the apostles in 1 Corinthians 11:23–25 show that he is making them the first priests and instituting Holy Orders?

3. Read John 13:12–17. What is Jesus telling the apostles about their priestly vocation?

YOU Chat

1. What does St. Thomas mean when he says, "Only Christ [is] truly priest. But the others are his ministers" (p. 143, margin)?

2. St. John Vianney says, "If someone wants to destroy religion, he begins by attacking priests" (p. 144, margin). Why would that be so?

3. St. Ignatius of Antioch says we must all follow the lead of the bishop (p. 145, margin). Why does he say that?

YOU Challenge

Pray: Ask God for priestly vocations, for men who will answer the call to serve Christ's Church in holiness of life as ordained ministers.

Support: Uphold the Bishop of Rome (the Pope), your local bishop, and your pastor with prayer and obedience.

The Sacraments of Communion and Mission—Holy Orders and Marriage

Topic 8: You Were Made for Me; I Was Made for You

Behind YOUCAT

When Stevie Wonder sang, "I was made to love her", and when Maroon 5 sings, "And she will be loved", everyone knows what they're singing about. Man was made for woman, and woman for man. And love wasn't made just for a day. Deep in our hearts all of us want to be loved exclusively, totally, and always. The closest thing in this world to fulfilling this longing is married love. "A man shall leave his mother and a woman leave her home; they shall travel on to where the two shall be as one" are lyrics from the *Wedding Song*. They express well the reality of the covenant of marriage. Even though we were made for this love, our fallen selfish selves can't get it done, not without some divine help. That help is on the way for those who willingly and freely give and receive the holy sacrament of Matrimony. Without it, most of us end up with one of those "she left me, he left me, I can't go on" or "hey, there lonely girl, lonely boy", broken-hearted love songs. That's not what we were made for. God has something much better in mind.

Read YOUCAT

Read nos. 260–261, 263–264, and 271.

What Does YOUCAT Say?

1. How do a man and a woman come to be married (nos. 260–261)?
2. Why is marriage indissoluble (no. 263)?
3. What threatens marriage; what renews marriage (no. 264)?
4. How does a family, built on a sacramental marriage, become an island of living faith (no. 271, and the margins of pp. 154–155)?

YOU Reflect

Do you believe in love? All of us long for love, and long to love and be loved. God, who is love, knows how we can best experience and share his love during this earthly pilgrimage. He made woman for man and vice versa. Because of this, many of us will be called to marriage, and a call to Christian marriage is a call to love another person with a total commitment to the very end. Even though man and woman are disposed to one another by God's creation, God does not call everyone to marriage. Many he calls to remain unmarried "for the sake of the kingdom" (Lk 18:29). Religious, celibate priests, and chaste, single lay people are free to work full-time for Christ, and to be fruitful through their service to others. Those called to remain celibate give up sexual activity so they can devote their energies to other things. But they are still called to a life full of love.

continued next page

What Does the Bible Say?

1. What inspired advice does St. Paul give to married couples in Ephesians 5:21–33? How is Christian marriage a sign of Christ's love for his Church?
2. How does Ruth's promise to her mother-in-law in Ruth 1:16–17 echo the promises Christian spouses make to one another?
3. Read Matthew 19:4–9. What does Jesus have to say about the indissolubility of marriage?
4. How does John 2:1–11 intimately link Christian marriage with the love of Christ and our obedience to him?

YOU Chat

1. Why do you think Kierkegaard says, "Love is perfected in fidelity" (p. 150, margin)?
2. Comment on the statement: "Absolute fidelity in marriage is not so much a human achievement as it is a testimony to the faithfulness of God" (YOUCAT, no. 263). Why is *absolute* truth and loyalty so important on this earth, where so much is *relative*?
3. Comment on these two statements found in the margin of page 151: "To love a person means to see him as God intended him" (Fyodor M. Dostoyevsky), and "To love someone means to be the only one to see a miracle that is invisible to others" (Francois Mauriac). What do you think is the meaning of true love between a man and a woman?

YOU Challenge

Pray: Every day ask that God will show you your vocation and prepare you for it. Pray for the same things for your future spouse, if God is calling you to marriage.

Ask: Turn to Mary, the Mother of God, and request her prayers for you to receive and live the virtues of purity and modesty in your daily life.

Contribute: Support your family or the family of God, the Church. Do one thing this week above and beyond your usual duties, to make things better for your family or your parish.

1. What special challenges do highly active, committed people face in married life, especially when it comes to their family life and their careers? Which must have priority?
2. What problems do you think our society's emphasis on sexual expression creates for people to live chastely and to use their sexuality well?

Other Liturgical Celebrations

Topic 9: Accessorize

Behind YOUCAT

Once you have the basics, there is room to "accessorize", even in the Church. Even though we are called to one faith, it is not just "one size fits all". God and his Church provide us with many ways to receive and cooperate with grace, many ways to be empowered for good and protected from evil, including sacramentals, exorcisms, the veneration of relics, participation in pilgrimages, and the practice of the Stations of the Cross. Even when we have died, the Church provides for us a Christian funeral and burial for the benefit of the dead and to express the reality that we die in Christ in order to rise with him.

Read YOUCAT

Read nos. 272–278.

What Does YOUCAT Say?

1. Why are sacramentals such a powerful help in the spiritual life (no. 272)?
2. Does Jesus have power over demons? Does his Church? What is an exorcism (no. 273)?
3. What does popular piety include (nos. 274–276)?
4. What are the Stations of the Cross (no. 277)?
5. Why is a Christian funeral and burial so important (no. 278)?

YOU Reflect

Sacramentals do not cause to happen what they signify, as sacraments do. But they can dispose us for the graces God wants to give, provided we use them with faith in God. Do you know of the powerful effects of wearing with faith a miraculous medal, a St. Benedict medal, or the scapular (just to name a few)? Have you ever venerated a holy relic and experienced the inspiration of knowing a "friend of God" who is thinking of you and praying for you that you will have God's mighty help to overcome evil and do lasting good in your life?

1. It is superstition to attribute to some natural object a supernatural power. How are the things the Bible describes in Luke 8:44, Acts 5:15, and Acts 19:11–12 different from superstition? What additional elements are at work?
2. Why should a Christian have both sorrow and joy at the Christian funeral of a friend or family member?
3. Sacramentals are sometimes associated with popular piety. Do you think there can be dangers involved with popular piety as well as benefits? Explain your answer.

What Does the Bible Say?

1. Read Matthew 10:1, which shows Jesus exercising his authority over evil spirits. Then read 1 Peter 5:8–9, which reminds us of the continued threat of the devil in the world. How is Jesus' power over evil exercised today in his Church?
2. Prayerfully read Luke 23:24–53 and then, in your own words, tell what benefit Christians receive by following Jesus on his Way of the Cross.

YOU Chat

1. Have you ever participated in a religious procession, made a pilgrimage, or venerated a relic of a saint? How can these examples of popular piety help lead us to Christ?
2. Why are Christian funerals and burials so important?
3. What sacramentals have you used? Can you recommend any to a fellow Christian?

YOU Challenge

Discover: Find out when the next funeral will be held in your parish Church, attend it, and pray for the dearly departed person.

Follow: Accompany Jesus on his Way of the Cross some Friday this month. It's a powerful and ancient devotion that helps us carry our own cross in life (no. 277).

Go: Approach your parish priest and have him bless your rosary or a holy picture you have, and use that blessed article with faith.

PART 3

HOW WE ARE TO HAVE LIFE IN CHRIST— LIVING LIFE TO THE FULLEST

Why We Are Put on Earth, What We Are Supposed to Do, and How God's Holy Spirit Helps Us to Do It

Topic 1: Everybody's Fancy

Behind YOUCAT

When your parents were young, they probably watched Mr. Rogers on TV and heard him sing, "Everybody's fancy, everybody's fine; your body's fancy, so is mine." A kid's song? Sure. But that doesn't stop it from telling us something true. God made the human person, body and soul, very "fancy" indeed. God made us in his own image and for a divine purpose. Since God is love, we must be made for love. Since God is eternally and supremely happy, that's what we are made for, too. Since God is perfect goodness, beauty, and truth, he gave us satisfaction in seeking and finding the good, the beautiful, and the true. And that's why he made us free, so we can choose love, happiness, goodness, truth, and beauty now and forever! Every human person—no matter how young, old, limited, unattractive, lonely, or poor—was made for love, made for God. All morality really involves this: love every human person, no matter what it takes, no matter what it costs.

Read YOUCAT

Read nos. 279–280, 283, 285–287, 290–292, 295, and 297.

What Does YOUCAT Say?
1. What role do faith and the sacraments play in living a good life (no. 279)?
2. Why does every human person, from the first moment of life in the womb, have awesome and built-in dignity (no. 280)?
3. What are the Beatitudes, and what have they to do with our happiness (nos. 283 and 285, and p. 164, Pascal quote)?
4. What is freedom, and what is it for (nos. 286, 287, and 290)?

continued next page

YOU Reflect

Why were you put on earth? God made you a unique and unrepeatable individual—a person. What is each of us supposed to do with this precious gift of life given us by God? "Seek, and you will find" (Mt 7:7), says Christ. All who sincerely seek, find, step by step, the answer to the question "Why am I here?" But, when we find out, are we willing to live accordingly? That's the great question.

1. Why do you suppose some people seem to take a long time to find their purpose in life, if they ever find it?
2. Have ever asked the Lord about your purpose in life? Have you asked him to guide you in finding your life's calling?

5. Do the ends justify the means (nos. 291–292)?

6. What is conscience, and how does one form a right conscience (nos. 295 and 297)?

What Does the Bible Say?

1. John 15:4–5 tells us the foundation of all Christian morality. What is it?

2. Jesus gave us his Beatitudes in Matthew 5:3–12. What's in it for us if we live according to the Beatitudes?

3. St. John teaches us in 1 John 3:1–3 the source of our human dignity and the destiny for which God created each of us. What is the source of our dignity; what is our destiny?

4. What does St. Paul say about Christian freedom in Romans 8:15?

YOU Chat

1. On page 162 of YOUCAT, St. Teresa of Avila gives us very good advice. Read what she has to say; what do you think would happen if many more people in the world followed her advice?

2. Pope Benedict points out that when God disappears from human society, man is greatly reduced. Why do you think that is the case? How do we invite God back into our lives?

3. Brother Roger says that the source of our happiness lies in communion with God. Do you agree with him? Why, or why not?

YOU Challenge

Pray: Each day, several times, pray: "Jesus, I trust in you. You are enough for me."

Respect Life: Do something this week to help a younger sibling, a grandparent, or a neighbor who needs your help. Jesus says, "As you did it not to one of the least of these, you did it not to me" (Mt 25:45).

The Dignity of the Human Person

Topic 2: Virtue Is Its Own Reward

Behind YOUCAT

Have you ever had a friend—at least you thought he was your friend—who you found out later told other people lies about you? Or have you known someone who seemed to be very friendly to you when you were around, but you found out later, he was always putting you down? Sometimes we have to learn the hard way who our real friends are. You can't be a friend unless you practice virtue, and your trust in anyone who claims to be a friend but isn't virtuous will prove to be misplaced. Sooner or later you will get burned. There is no true friendship without the practice of virtue.

Virtue is the habit of doing good. Some virtues we acquire by repeatedly doing good acts (natural virtues), but some we can only get if God gives them to us (supernatural virtues). No matter how we get them, we've got to use them, or they do us no good. The main advice Dale Carnegie gave in his famous, best-selling book, *How to Win Friends and Influence People*, was you can't win a friend without being a good friend yourself, and you can't influence people for the good unless you learn to practice virtue.

Read YOUCAT

Read nos. 299, 301–311, 313–314, 316, and 318.

YOU Reflect

God blesses us with many gifts and virtues. The three that abide are faith, hope, and charity. And "the greatest of these is charity." This truth is so all-powerful that St. Augustine goes so far as to say, "Love, and do what you will." God, who is love, has made us in his image. Will you search for his gifts and the virtues that bring abundant life and love? Will you practice them faithfully?

1. Sometimes we think that as long as we mean well, we can do whatever we want. Do you think that this is what St. Augustine meant when he said, "Love, and do what you will"?

2. Why do you think that charity—love of God and love of neighbor because we love God—is "greater" than faith and hope?

What Does YOUCAT Say?

1. How do we become virtuous people (nos. 299–306)?
2. What is faith, what is hope, and what is charity (nos. 305–309)?
3. What are the seven gifts of the Holy Spirit (no. 310)?
4. What are the twelve fruits of the Holy Spirit (no. 311)?
5. How do we know God's mercy is one of his most important attributes (nos. 313–314)?
6. Are all sins the same in seriousness (no. 316)?
7. What are vices (no. 318)?

What Does the Bible Say?

1. According to 1 Corinthians 13:1–13, what are the virtues that abide forever?
2. What reasons does St. John give in 1 John 2:3–6 for obeying Christ's commandments?

YOU Chat

1. It's often said that nobody's perfect. Yet Jesus says, "You, therefore, must be perfect, as your heavenly Father is perfect" (Mt 5:48). How is that possible?
2. The word "cardinal" comes from the Latin "cardo", meaning "hinge". How are cardinal virtues like hinges?
3. How can we become more devoted to and dependent on the Holy Spirit to live a gifted life of virtue?

YOU Challenge

Learn: Memorize the cardinal virtues, supernatural virtues, and the gifts of the Holy Spirit.

Pray: Ask the Holy Spirit at least once a day to increase his sevenfold gifts within you.

Love: Each day look for opportunities to perform an act of service out of love for a family member, friend, or stranger.

Human Community

Topic 3: The Lonesome End

Behind YOUCAT

Years ago, the Army football team used to run an offense with one *wide out*, way at the end of the line, just a few feet from the sideline. He never joined the team in the huddle. He just stayed out there and somehow learned his role in the play, though how he knew what to do, most fans never found out. He came to be known as *The Lonesome End*.

God designed us for fellowship. He wants us to "huddle up", learn the play, and run it together as a team. No "lonesome ends" in his design (unless you want to count hermits). Since by God's design we need one another, it's of absolute importance that we "strengthen" the "brethren" (Lk 22:32), as Jesus commanded Peter.

We can't successfully live this life alone; each person, inestimably valuable in himself, needs to live in solidarity with every other person, or it all falls apart. Unfortunately, we often experience things falling apart and breaking down because of our own sinfulness. But God does not abandon us; he has sent his Holy Spirit to bind us together in Christ.

Read YOUCAT

Read nos. 321, 323–324, 329–330, 333–334, 337–339, and 342.

YOU Reflect

Blessed John Paul II said, "No one can claim, as Cain did, that he is not responsible for the fate of his brother." Together we form a human family of individual persons. When those persons respect and love one another, then freedom, peace, and security are the outcome for all the members of the human family. Furthermore, according to St. Catherine of Siena, God says: "I have willed that one should need another and that all should be my ministers in distributing the graces and gifts they have received from me."

What Does YOUCAT Say?

1. What are the four central principles of Catholic social teaching (p. 181, margin, and nos. 323–324)?
2. All justice is based on respect for each person's human dignity, but are all men equal (nos. 329–330)?
3. What is natural law, and how can we know it (nos. 333–334)?
4. How are we saved (no. 337)?
5. Discuss the mysterious reality of grace, and how it works in us (nos. 338–339).

What Does the Bible Say?

1. Do you think Acts 5:29 proposes a sound principle for social justice?
2. How is Matthew 25:40 the basis of all social justice?
3. According to St. Paul in Ephesians 2:8–10, how are faith, grace, and good works related? Who made us for good works?
4. What does St. Peter in his first letter (1 Pt 1:14–16) affirm about the Christian calling? How can we sinners successfully answer that call?

YOU Chat

1. What do you think is more important, society or the individual? Give reasons for your answer.
2. Why is personhood a foundational principle for all justice in society?
3. What is subsidiarity, and how can we practice it in our own lives and in society?

YOU Challenge

Love: Do one good, but unannounced, act today for a member of your family.

Memorize: Commit to memory these words of Pope Benedict XVI: "Each of us is the result of a thought of God. Each of us is willed, each of us is loved, each of us is necessary" (Homily for the Mass of Inauguration of the Pontificate of Benedict XVI, April 24, 2005).

Learn: Study the meaning of each of the four central principles of Catholic Social Teaching: personhood, the common good, solidarity, and subsidiarity.

The Church

Topic 4: You Can't Give What You Don't Have

Behind YOUCAT

Advertisers are always making promises, but can they really deliver? Buy the car, and you'll get the girl. Eat at this fast-food place, and you'll be surrounded by smiling, laughing friends, never alone again. Happiness, satisfaction, love, an end to loneliness—there is nothing on earth that can give you these things, except the Church. And the reason the Church can give you these is because the Church exists to give you Jesus, the fulfillment of all our desires.

"Even today the Church gives me Jesus. That says it all", said Jesuit Henri Cardinal de Lubac. The Church, by God's grace, bridges all that threatens to separate us from really knowing Jesus. Time and space are no obstacle. Trials and sorrows cannot keep us away. Even sin and death are overcome. In the Church, we hear Jesus speak, receive his forgiveness, are fed by him in the Eucharist. We are freely given a share in the life of Christ so that we, in turn, can go out and give freely what we have received.

Read YOUCAT

Read nos. 343–344 and 347.

What Does YOUCAT Say?

1. What does the Church do for us (nos. 343–344)?
2. What is hypocrisy, and what's the cure for it (no. 347)?

YOU Reflect

Henri Cardinal de Lubac asks, "What would I know about [Jesus], what connection would there be between him and me without the Church?"[1] It is only the Church that can give us Jesus. We, in turn, as faithful members of the Church, are privileged to give Jesus to everyone we meet.

1. Identify some ways in which the Church makes Jesus present to you.
2. Name some ways in which you make Jesus present to others.

---

[1] In *Mysterium Fidei*, Pope Paul VI teaches there are seven different ways in which Jesus, as God and man, is present in the Church.

What Does the Bible Say?

1. In 1 Corinthians 12:27, St. Paul tells us why we must be members of the Church if we are to belong to Christ. What reason does St. Paul give?
2. In Luke 10:16, we hear Christ giving his own authority to whom? Why did he do that? Is Christ's authority still operative in our world today?

YOU Chat

1. Blaise Pascal (p. 190, margin) advises those who want to come to believe to "do everything that the faith requires, as though you were already a believer." Do you think that strategy will work?
2. What does a hypocritical person do? How can we avoid hypocrisy in our lives? Should we be quick to accuse others of hypocrisy? Why, or why not?
3. Do you think someone will continue to be a believing Catholic if he seldom participates in Sunday Mass? Why, or why not?

YOU Challenge

Memorize: Learn and live the Five Precepts of the Church.

Pray: Intercede this week for Catholics who have stopped living their faith; pray they come home to the family of God.

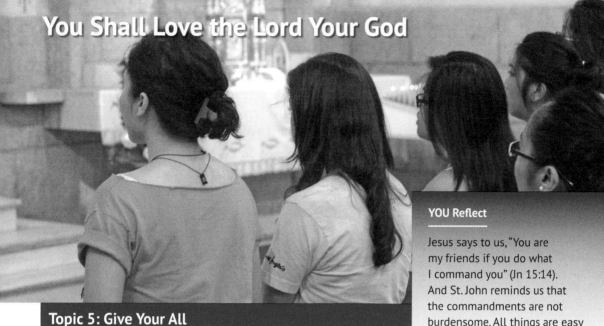

You Shall Love the Lord Your God

Topic 5: Give Your All

Behind YOUCAT

In *Star Wars*, when Yoda trained Luke Skywalker to be a Jedi, he said, "There is no *try*; do, or do not." Likewise, God does not command us to try to love him, to give it our best shot. NO. The Old Testament says, and Jesus himself repeats, "You shall love the LORD your God with all your heart, and with all your soul, and with all your might" (Deut 6:5; see Mk 12:30). Yoda wanted Luke to give his whole being to the task at hand, and then only would it be done; God wants us to give our *all*, and then we cannot fail to love. It is not simply a "force" at work within us. It is God himself that loves through us. When we take this first step to love, it follows naturally that we will strive to obey all of God's laws of love.

Read YOUCAT

Read nos. 348–349, 352–353, 355, 359–360, and 364–365.

What Does YOUCAT Say?

1. What does Jesus say we must do to have eternal life and to remain in him (no. 348)?

2. What are the Ten Commandments (no. 349 and the margins of pp. 192–193)?

3. What must be the absolute priority in our life if we are to fulfill the destiny for which we are made: possessing truth and happiness (nos. 352–353)?

4. What is forbidden by the First Commandment (no. 355)?

5. What is protected by the Second Commandment (no. 359)?

continued next page

6. Why do Christians make the Sign of the Cross (no. 360)?

7. How and why do Christians make Sunday "the Lord's day" (nos. 364–365)?

What Does the Bible Say?

1. Read Exodus 20:2–17 and Deuteronomy 5:6–21. These texts are the basis of what?

2. What powerful motivation do St. John and the Holy Spirit give us in 1 John 4:16–21 for keeping the commandments of God?

3. How does Psalm 113 inspire us to keep the Second Commandment?

YOU Chat

1. If reason can know the obligations listed in the Ten Commandments, why did God bother to reveal them to us?

2. Aren't the Ten Commandments outmoded? They are at least four thousand years old; what have they to do with us?

3. What happens to the person who wholeheartedly worships God? Is he changed in some way? How?

YOU Challenge

Memorize: Learn the Ten Commandments by heart (no. 349).

Love: Make one sacrifice today out of love for your mom or dad.

Visit: Pay a visit to Jesus in the Blessed Sacrament. Spend at least ten minutes in adoration in obedience to the First Commandment. After all, he is God; there is no other.

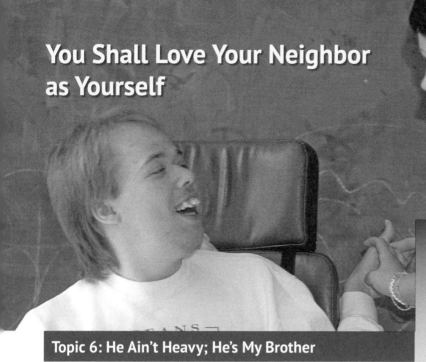

You Shall Love Your Neighbor as Yourself

Topic 6: He Ain't Heavy; He's My Brother

Behind YOUCAT

You may not remember the music group The Hollies or their megahit, "He Ain't Heavy; He's My Brother". It's worth checking out on the Internet or elsewhere. And the old hymn "Let There Be Peace on Earth" tells us, "With God as our Father, brothers all are we; let me walk with my brother in perfect harmony. . . ." Yes, we are all children of our loving Father God, which makes us all sisters and brothers of one another. Jesus tells us his burden is easy; his yoke is light (see Mt 11:30). It is the burden of love of neighbor; it is the yoke of justice and peace. Cain asked God, "Am I my brother's keeper?" (Gen 4:9). For those who follow Christ, the answer is a clear and resounding: YES! As far as it is in my power to desire and intend what is good for my fellow man, that is what I am commanded to do. The Church helps us apply the idea of loving our neighbor to different circumstances, beginning with following the commandments.

Read YOUCAT

Read nos. 367–368, 371, 378–379, 383, and 395.

What Does YOUCAT Say?

1. What does the Fourth Commandment say about what we owe to our parents and others in rightful authority (nos. 367 and 371–373)?
2. In God's plan, how important is the family (nos. 368–370)?
3. What does the Fifth Commandment forbid and why (nos. 378–379 and 383)?
4. What is peace (no. 395)?

What Does the Bible Say?

1. According to Sirach 7:27–28, can we ever repay God or our parents for what they have given us?

2. St. Paul teaches family members and members of the Church how to love one another in Romans 12:10 and Colossians 3:21. What does St. Paul say?

3. How does Jesus elevate the Fifth Commandment in Matthew 5:21–22?

YOU Chat

1. What will it take to renew family life in the world today?

2. If the laws of every State protected innocent human life from conception to natural death, how would the world change?

3. How are peace and justice related to one another?

YOU Challenge

Love: Hug your mom today and tell her you love her. If she's far away, give her a "phone hug". Or pray for her.

Love Life: Choose a pro-life activity and participate in it, such as "Life Chain" or a pro-life march. To find out what God wants you to do to help mothers and their prenatal children, contact your parish respect life committee.

You Shall Love Your Neighbor as Yourself

Topic 7: Operate according to the Manual

Behind YOUCAT

Cars come with owner's manuals, which are best followed if we expect the car to run smoothly and successfully. God has given mankind a "manual", the Ten Commandments, by which we are to live our lives. When human beings operate their lives according to the commandments, society runs smoothly. If not, we experience breakdowns, crashes, and serious injury. Everyone alive today has suffered as a result of someone not following the "manual". Consider the suffering that can come from unfaithfulness in marriage—suffering to one's parents, someone in the extended family, or close friends. And all of us at one time or another have experienced a violation of our own personal property, or have failed to receive a just reward for our work. In a world in which people don't "follow the directions", we can be part of the problem or part of the solution. If we operate according to the God-given human being "manual", the Ten Commandments, we'll certainly be part of the solution.

Read YOUCAT

Read nos. 402–404, 407, 415–421, 424–425, 428, 440, 445, and 450–451.

What Does YOUCAT Say?

1. What is the significance of married love (no. 402)?
2. How are the gifts of human sexuality and love related to one another (nos. 402–404 and 407)?

continued next page

YOU Reflect

Two of the greatest human goods—faithful married love and wealth—Jesus freely sacrificed, among other reasons, as a sign of his total love for each one of us. Married love is created to be a free, total, exclusive, self-giving of one man to one woman and of one woman to one man. It is the most profound and beautiful of all human loves, but Christ's total self-giving to each of us is even more beautiful and rich: "Though he was rich, yet for your sake he became poor, so that by his poverty you might become rich" (2 Cor 8:9).

1. What does it say about how important married love and wealth are that Jesus gave them up? Does this indicate that they are completely unimportant or that they are important? Explain.
2. Have you ever given up something you greatly treasured? How did it make you feel? Did you experience freedom? Why or why not?

3. What is the Church's judgment on homosexuality, and how are we to truly love all persons, including those who describe themselves as homosexual (no. 415)?

4. What are the four essential elements of a Christian marriage (nos. 416–418)?

5. Why does the Church support natural family planning and oppose contraception and sterilization (nos. 418–421)?

6. What is adultery? Can Catholics divorce (no. 424)?

7. Why does the Church strongly urge us to resist the societal pressure for couples to live together without being married (no. 425)?

8. What is forbidden by the Seventh Commandment (no. 428)?

9. Are Christians obliged to become involved in politics and society (no. 440)?

10. Explain the meaning of the principle "labor before capital," espoused by Blessed John Paul II (no. 445).

What Does the Bible Say?

1. What do Genesis 2:18 and 2:24 teach us about man and woman?

2. What does Ecclesiastes 5:10 have to say about money?

3. What does Jesus say about our treasure in Matthew 6:21?

YOU Chat

1. Comment on and discuss this statement with your friends: "Love is the free self-giving of the heart" (no. 402).

2. When are sexual relations a lie? When do they express the truth?

3. How is the right to private property only a relative right and not an absolute right?

YOU Challenge

Read: Look up Song of Songs 8:6–7 and 1 Timothy 4:4, and take time to reflect on how good and beautiful God considers married love.

Pray: Intercede for your future spouse and yourself (assuming God is calling you to marriage). Ask God to prepare you both for faithfulness and holiness in your married life.

You Shall Love Your Neighbor as Yourself

Topic 8: Truth? What Is That?

Behind YOUCAT

Lots of people today have Pontius Pilate's attitude toward the truth. When Pilate asked Jesus if he was a king, Jesus replied, "For this I have come into the world, to bear witness to the truth. Every one who is of the truth hears my voice." Pilate said to Jesus, "What is truth?" (Jn 18:37–38). Skeptics today ask the same question, especially when it comes to moral truth—the truth of right and wrong. Jesus also said that the truth would set us free (see Jn 8:32). By this statement, he meant freedom from falsehood and deception. When it comes to right and wrong, the truth is essential and liberating. God's commandments aren't just rules—they're about *the truth*, about what is *really* good and *really* bad for us. When we live according to his commandments, we're abiding or living *in the truth*.

Read YOUCAT

Read nos. 452–454, 458, 462–463, and 466.

What Does YOUCAT Say?

1. The Eighth Commandment teaches us not to lie; what does our relationship to the truth have to do with our relationship with God (nos. 452–453)?

2. How strong must our commitment to the truth of the faith be (no. 454)?

3. How confidential is the secret of the confessional (no. 458)?

4. How can we achieve the "purity of heart" commanded by the Ninth Commandment (nos. 462–463)?

continued next page

YOU Reflect

The *Rule of St. Benedict*, written by the great saint and Father of the Church, states: "Hate no one. Do not be jealous. Do not act out of envy. Do not love quarreling. Flee arrogance." It takes humility to act in this way. Humility doesn't mean thinking less of yourself than is really the case. It means seeing yourself as you really are in relation to the all-powerful God—honestly recognizing your God-given talents, as well as your limitations, weaknesses, and sins. When we are humble, we are able to repent and ask God's help overcoming hatred, jealousy, envy, quarrelling, and arrogance. Free of these evils, we are able to enjoy what is really important.

1. Do you think of yourself as humble? Why or why not?

2. What is the relationship between humility and truth?

3. How does the sacrament of Reconciliation help us grow in humility?

5. How does one achieve "purity of heart" (no. 463)?

6. Why is envy something we should fight against (no. 466)?

What Does the Bible Say?

1. In Matthew 6:21, what does Jesus say about the human heart and our treasure?

2. St. Paul says in Colossians 3:5 that there is something we must "put to death". What is it?

3. What does Jesus say we should "beware of" in Luke 12:15?

YOU Chat

1. If people spoke the truth and respected each other's human dignity and rightful property, how would our society function?

2. Is it ever okay to lie? What about the extreme case when to tell the truth might cost someone else his innocent life?

3. It is good to study the moral law presented in YOUCAT in detail. There is much to think about and much to help you know what is right. At the same time, can you think of a simple way to sum up all God's commandments?

YOU Challenge

Pray: Say to the Lord three times today, "Jesus, meek and humble of heart, make our hearts like yours."

Meditate: Think of the gifts God has given to one of your friends, gifts you are happy your friend possesses, and thank God for blessing your friend with those gifts.

Acknowledge: Think of a quality a friend or family member has which you lack. Tell your friend or family member how much you admire that quality in him.

PART 4

HOW WE SHOULD PRAY— ENTERING THE GREAT DIALOGUE

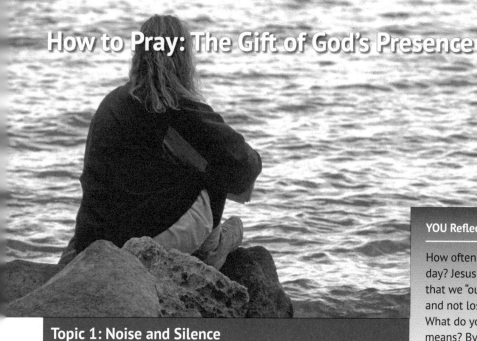

How to Pray: The Gift of God's Presence

Topic 1: Noise and Silence

Behind YOUCAT

Have you ever been in the country far from the noise of the city, away from cell phones, CDs, DVDs, TVs, and all the other clatter? If you ever have been in a place where there is deep silence—no hums, chirps, or human racket—you may have experienced that silence like a presence. Of course, we don't have to run off to a desert every time we want to pray or experience the presence of God. But, as in every other relationship, we need to be attentive and listening, ready to hear and to respond. That can be hard to do if we're always immersed in a world of noise. Jesus frequently went off into a deserted place or to a high mountain to commune with his Father. The heart of the Christian life is to follow Jesus' example—a life lived in the presence of God. All who seek God in prayer find him. If you want to follow Christ, you must never be afraid to escape the noise and seek God in the silence of prayer.

Read YOUCAT

Read no. 469–470, 474, 476, and 478.

What Does YOUCAT Say?

1. How would you define prayer (no. 469)?
2. What prompts us to pray? Why are we moved to do so (no. 470)?
3. How did Jesus pray, and how can we learn to pray from him (nos. 475–478)?

YOU Reflect

How often do you pray? Every day? Jesus said to his followers that we "ought always to pray and not lose heart" (Lk 18:1). What do you think the Lord means? By his example and teaching, Jesus left no doubt of the absolute importance of prayer. Yet, without his help and the help of the Holy Spirit, often we don't even know how to begin. This is why the first disciples said, "Lord, teach us to pray" (Lk 11:1).

1. Do you ever feel like you want to pray, but you don't know what to say? Why or why not?
2. Are you comfortable or uncomfortable praying in your own words rather than a "set prayer"? Why?
3. How can a "set prayer" be helpful to our praying?
4. How often do you pray without asking for something? Do you ever simply thank God or acknowledge his goodness?

What Does the Bible Say?

1. Read Luke 11:1–4 and Matthew 6:7–15. How does Jesus teach us to pray?
2. Read Psalm 4. How do we know God hears our prayer? How can we learn to hear him and trust him?
3. Read Acts 17:24–28. Why is it reasonable and virtuous to ask God for what we need?

YOU Chat

1. What has silence to do with prayer?
2. St. Augustine says, "Do what you can, and pray for what you cannot, and so God will grant you the ability to do it." What do you think he meant?
3. What does it mean to say that "prayer is a gift one obtains through prayer"?

YOU Challenge

Ask: Every morning ask God to teach you to pray this day, to increase your desire to pray, and to give you the gift of prayer.

Pray: Sit down in a quiet place for ten minutes each day with the New Testament or Brother Lawrence's *Practice of the Presence of God* or YOUCAT, and place yourself in God's presence, then listen to what he says from the book or in your heart.

Write: After praying, write a one-sentence resolution based on what you heard: "Today I will _____."

Practice: When you can, throughout your day, *remember* God. Momentarily lift your heart to him in love.

How to Pray: The Gift of God's Presence

Topic 2: YES!

Behind YOUCAT

Long before they learn to say Yes, toddlers often know how to say No. If you don't think this is so, spend time with one-, two-, or even three-year-olds and count the number of times they say No. Of course, "No" is not all bad. In fact, there are plenty of things in the world to which our best and safest response would be a resounding "NO!" But that never applies to God. As Mary, the Mother of God and our Mother, teaches us, when it comes to God, we should always have the prayerful attitude of "YES!" She teaches us, in her last recorded words in the Gospel, to do whatever her Son tells us to do (Jn 2:5), which is always to say Yes in word and deed to the will of God the Father.

Read YOUCAT

Read nos. 479–481, 483, and 485–488.

What Does YOUCAT Say?

1. What is an important lesson about prayer that we can learn from Mary (no. 479)?
2. What are the five main types of prayer (no. 483)?
3. What does standing in prayer represent? What does kneeling represent (no. 486)?
4. What reasons did Blessed John Paul II give for saying the Rosary was his favorite prayer (p. 265, margin)?

YOU Reflect

How's your prayer life? That's a question you may never have been asked in your entire life, but it's also a question we can't be afraid to ask our Catholic and Christian friends. In fact, if you find a friend who is bold enough to ask you that question and help you stay on track in a life of daily prayer, well, then you have found a friend indeed.

Prayer does not come naturally to us fallen human beings. Adam used to "walk in the Garden with God" (see Gen 3:8). That's the biblical analogy used to say that Adam naturally and easily conversed with God. But one of the first and most devastating losses caused by the sin of Adam is that prayer does not come naturally; it's a struggle, a battle, a work that requires the grace of God and a humble heart, willing to persevere. And we need our Christian friends to encourage us to stay the course, and we, in turn, need to encourage them. So, how's your prayer life?

continued next page

What Does the Bible Say?

1. How do St. Gabriel and St. Elizabeth teach us to pray in Luke 1:26–45?
2. What does St. Paul tell us about Jesus and intercessory prayer in Romans 8:34–35?
3. St. Paul has more advice about prayer in Colossians 4:2. What does he say about perseverance and thanksgiving in prayer?

YOU Chat

1. What would you say to someone who has never prayed the Rosary but is open to finding out about it?
2. How is Mary's Yes to God the model of all Christian prayer?
3. What attitudes should we expect a Christian to have when praying?

YOU Challenge

Pray: Recite the Rosary today with your family or with a friend.

Ask: Turn to Mary, our Mother, each day, and ask her to teach you how to pray as she does.

Memorize: Learn the Mysteries of the Rosary.

1. What obstacles to prayer do you find in your life?
2. How would your friends react if you asked them about their prayer lives? Would you be embarrassed to do so? Why or why not?
3. Do you think it helpful to pray as a family? Explain your answer.

The Sources of Prayer

Topic 3: Unremembered

Behind YOUCAT

Were you ever introduced to someone whom you liked immediately, remembered the person's name, and looked forward to getting to know him? Yet, the next few times you see him, it seems he doesn't know you from Adam, and he certainly doesn't remember your name? It hurts to be forgotten, unrecognized, unremembered. With God, it's never that way. He has known us since before we were. He called us out of nothingness into being. He thinks of us constantly. We're precious to him; he calls us by name. In fact, he knows our secret name, the one we will be known by in eternity, the one that captures the very essence of who we are, really. Since he remembers us constantly, doesn't it seem right that we should think of him from time to time at least, speak to him, call him by name? Prayer is remembering God who loves us is here, and he is loving us right now!

Read YOUCAT

Read nos. 491–493 and 496–498.

What Does YOUCAT Say?

1. What do Kierkegaard, Simone Weil, St. Augustine, and Blessed Mother Teresa of Calcutta say about prayer (pp. 270 and 271, margins)?
2. What is the relationship between personal prayer and the prayer of the Church (no. 492)?
3. List three of the characteristics of Christian prayer (no. 493).
4. Who helps us pray (nos. 496 and 497)?
5. Where should we pray (no. 498)?

What Does the Bible Say?

1. Psalm 40:1 tells us we must wait patiently if we are to pray. Why is that so?
2. In Romans 8:26, St. Paul tells us we are helped to pray by whom?

YOU Chat

1. Why must we pray?
2. What can we do to learn how to pray?
3. On whom can we rely to teach us how to pray as we ought?

YOU Challenge

Meditate on God's Word: Each day read one verse from the Gospel and think about it deeply for ten minutes. Ask the Holy Spirit to speak to your heart.

Schedule: Make time for God. Build into your day a ten- to fifteen-minute prayer time.

Listen: Our Lord has a word just for you; open your heart and mind to hear and obey.

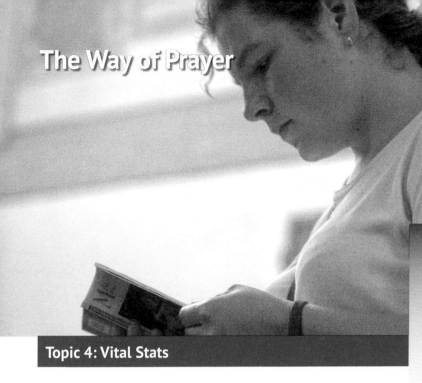

The Way of Prayer

Topic 4: Vital Stats

Behind YOUCAT

Your doctor may know a lot about you: your height, weight, birth date, immunization records, blood type, etc. The school office probably has filed away all your pertinent information, as well. For all of that, no one at the doctor's office or the school office knows you anywhere near as well as your best friend, even if your best friend doesn't happen to know all of your vital stats.

With God, it's no different. Some people take the time to learn a lot about him. They may read the Bible or YOUCAT or other religious works describing God. That's an important beginning, but it's not what satisfies. Interior meditation, savoring God's presence, listening to his heartbeat of love for you, that's what satisfies. Really getting to know God and getting to be his good friend is way more important than knowing some, or even a lot, of God's vital stats.

Read YOUCAT

Read nos. 500–503, 505, and 507–510.

What Does YOUCAT Say?

1. What are the three ways of prayer, and what is presupposed by each of them (nos. 500–503)?
2. Is prayer always easy or does it take effort (nos. 505 and 507–508, p. 273, margin, Bl. Teresa of Calcutta)?
3. How does prayer connect us with reality (no. 509)?
4. What is the most well-known formula of the ancient "Jesus prayer", which can help us pray always and remember we are in his holy presence today (no. 510)?

YOU Reflect

Have you ever really asked yourself, "Where does my life come from? How did I get here?" Although it's obvious we didn't make ourselves, often we act as if we did. We act like we own our lives. In reality, life "does not come from ourselves but from somewhere else" (p. 275, margin, Br. Roger Schutz). The many paths of prayer all have something in common. They are the ways we receive life from the Giver of all life: God.

1. How does prayer involve recognizing that we receive life as a gift, not as an accomplishment?
2. Are you ever afraid to think about God or matters of faith? Why or why not?

What Does the Bible Say?

1. What two things does James 4:2–3 teach us?

2. Explain what St. Paul teaches us in 1 Thessalonians 5:17–18 about how often and in what circumstances we should pray.

YOU Chat

1. Why is it we can't, or shouldn't, read the Bible like we read a newspaper or magazine? How should we "read" the Bible?

2. What can we do if we feel like prayer doesn't help?

3. What does a Christian accomplish through meditation? Would it be better if we were out there loving people rather than meditating?

YOU Challenge

Study: Investigate the three ways of prayer described in YOUCAT. How are they alike, and how do they differ?

Meditate: Try to meditate for ten minutes each day for a week, following the brief directions of YOUCAT, no. 502.

Read: Check out one of the many good books on prayer. You might start with Thomas Dubay's *Prayer Primer* or Peter Kreeft's *Prayer for Beginners*.

The Lord's Prayer: The Our Father

Topic 5: Children, Love Your Father

Behind YOUCAT

We can never love or thank our parents enough for the gift of life. Still, for some of us, our parents can be hard to love. A wise priest once said that being able to forgive our parents is a sign of maturity. Until we do, we can't fully grow up. Some people have trouble with their moms and others with their dads. Some have trouble with both. (Then, too, some people have never known their parents.) Let's focus on dads. If our dads weren't sinners like the rest of us, maybe they'd be easier to love. Yet, without a doubt, the good that fathers have to offer their children is something beautiful and precious, a dim reflection of the love and care of our perfect heavenly Father. And where dads fall short, we know that God our Father can make up the difference. He's only waiting for us to turn to him.

Read YOUCAT

Read nos. 511–515 and 517–521.

What Does YOUCAT Say?

1. Who taught the Our Father? Why (nos. 511–512)?
2. What is the structure of the Our Father? How many petitions does it include (no. 513)?
3. How important a prayer is the Our Father for Christians (no. 514)?
4. Are we actually God's children? Is he really our loving Father (nos. 515 and 517)?

continued next page

YOU Reflect

Human fathers are weak, sinful, imperfect, and sometimes cause great harm to their children, but at their best they can be protective, loving, strong and gentle, wise in a way that dimly reflects the perfect Fatherhood of God. God is much more *Father* than any human father could ever be. Jesus taught us to entrust ourselves to God our Father, to seek his plan for us, and to ask for all we need to be happy.

1. In what sense is God our Father?
2. When someone's father has failed, how can thinking about God the Father help?

5. Where is God the Father (no. 518)?

6. For what are we really asking when we say, "Hallowed be thy name, thy kingdom come, thy will be done on earth as it is in heaven" (nos. 519–521)?

What Does the Bible Say?

1. Read Matthew 6:9–13 and Luke 11:2–4. Are these presentations of the Lord's Prayer slightly different? If so, how so?

2. Read Colossians 3:2. How does the Lord's Prayer empower us to do what St. Paul exhorts?

YOU Chat

1. Why do you think the Our Father is considered the perfect prayer?

2. Since God is our Father, how does that affect our relationships with our fellow man?

3. Comment and discuss this statement of St. Hildegard of Bingen in light of the Our Father: "Heaven on earth is wherever people are filled with love for God, for their fellowmen, and for themselves" (p. 283, margin).

YOU Challenge

Pray: Each day this week pray the Our Father slowly, dwelling on one word or phrase at a time and asking the Holy Trinity to enlighten and inspire you with the goodness, beauty, truth, and meaning of the words.

Live: Strive to live as a child of our one Father in heaven this day, seeing each person as part of your family.

Ask: St. Joseph can be a father to you. Ask him to help your father and all fathers to be the best dads they can be.

The Lord's Prayer: The Our Father

Topic 6: I Need

Behind YOUCAT

Do you remember the movie *What About Bob?* If you've never seen it, it's hilarious. In one unforgettable scene Bob Wiley follows his therapist Leo Marvin to New Hampshire, where Dr. Marvin and his family are on vacation, and in the middle of the resort village street Bob begs the good doctor to see him: "I need, I need, I need, gimme, gimme, gimme!!!" Fortunately, there's no need for us to beg the divine physician. He knows our needs. But he does want us to ask for what we need—not for his sake but for ours. And he has even taught us how to ask.

Read YOUCAT

Read nos. 514 and 522–527.

What Does YOUCAT Say?

1. When we ask for "our daily bread" in the Our Father what all are we asking for (nos. 522–523 and p. 285, margin)?
2. How are the mercy we seek and the mercy we show others inseparable (no. 524)?
3. What do we mean when we ask the Lord to "lead us not into temptation, but deliver us from evil" (nos. 525–526)?
4. What happens when a person says "Amen" to his prayer, especially the Our Father (no. 527)?

YOU Reflect

When something seems so right, so perfect, people often shout, "Yes!" "Amen!" means "Yes!" or "So be it!" It makes sense that we would say "Amen!" to conclude our prayer. It's a way of making a firm commitment to the truth of what we have just prayed. In a way, our whole life should be a prayer—a gift given to God. At the end of life, we want to have lived in such a way as to be able to say "Amen!" to all that has happened. We want to have confident hope in God and our destiny with him. Try to remember the best day of your life. Picture it. Relive it in your memory. Now multiply the *joy* infinitely and the *time* eternally. That's the life our Father has prepared for us. *Amen!*

1. Have you ever heard something in church or read something connected with your faith that *made you want* to say "Amen!"? How is that different from just giving the expected response at the end of a prayer?
2. Why do you suppose young people are sometimes bashful about giving the responses at Mass? What can they do to overcome their bashfulness?

What Does the Bible Say?

1. What does St. Paul say that God desires for everyone (1 Tim 2:4)?
2. Explain how Luke 6:36 and 1 John 4:20 help us understand love, mercy, forgiveness, and God the Father.
3. In St. John's first letter (1 Jn 5:19) to whom does he say we belong? Under whose power and rule is this world for the time being?

YOU Chat

1. Jesus taught his disciples only one prayer, the Our Father. Why do you think our Lord only taught this one prayer?
2. St. Thomas Aquinas calls the Our Father "the most perfect prayer" (no. 514). Give some reasons why this prayer is considered "perfect".
3. Do you think it is wrong to ask God for things when we pray? Why or why not?

YOU Challenge

Think and Forgive: Each day take five minutes to think of those you have hurt and ask God to forgive you, and think of those who have hurt you and, no matter how you feel about them, choose to forgive them and ask God to bring his good into their lives.

Go: Attend Holy Mass on Sunday, and as you pray with all the congregation the Our Father, think of our family unity with all gathered there and all our brothers and sisters everywhere in the world, in purgatory, and in heaven.